Praise for Your Legacy of Love

"Brilliant book!"
Buzzine.com

"A valuable resource for any caring person . . ."
Dee Ann Ray, Clinton Daily news

"Adams does a first rate job in making the
topic of death more palatable."
Norm Goldman, Bookpleasures

"An insightful and emotion-evoking manual."
Val Spencer, Reader Views

"This book is a must for anyone who wants to reduce the
suffering for their surviving loved ones."
Roger Ford, President of Healing in America

"Gemini's book inspires and instructs with such warmth and
kindness that readers can't help but feel embraced."
Megory Anderson, Founder of The Sacred Dying Foundation

"I'd never realized that it could be fun, exciting even,
to consider what to leave my family after I die."
**Dr. Heidi Horsley, Adjunct Professor at Columbia
University School of Social Work**

"This heartfelt treasure should be in the hands of every parent,
grandparent, husband or wife who wants to leave
something more meaningful than money behind."
**Donna L. Schuurman, EdD, FT, Executive Director,
The Dougy Center for Grieving Childr** ̣ ̣ ̣ **ies**

D1302171

Publishing **Beyond** Boundaries
www.liveconsciouslynow.com

Also by Gemini Adams

*The Top 100 Recipes for Happy Kids: Keep Your
Child Alert, Focused and Active*

100 Recetas Sanas Para Niños

Your
Legacy
of Love

Realize **The Gift** in Goodbye

Gemini Adams

First published by Live Consciously Publishing in 2010.
www.liveconsciouslynow.com
Printed and bound in the United States.

For information regarding quantity discounts, please contact the sales office:
(1) 310 453 7711 or email: orders@liveconsciouslynow.com

Library of Congress Control Number: 2009904240

ISBN: 978-0615193755

This book is not intended to be taken as legal, medical, or any other professional service. The information provided is not a substitute for professional advice. If you require legal, medical, or other expert assistance, you should seek the services of a competent professional. The author, the publisher and their employees, and agents are not liable for any damages arising from, or in connection with the use of, or reliance, on any information contained in this book.

Every attempt has been made to trace accurate ownership of copyrighted material in this book. Errors and omissions will be corrected in subsequent editions, provided that notification is sent to the publisher. Grateful acknowledgement is made for permission to reprint:

Farewell with Love and Instructions. Written by Lizette Alvarez. Copyright © 2005 The New York Times. Reprinted with permission.

What Will Matter. Written by Michael Josephson.© 2008 Josephson Institute. Copyright Reprinted with permission. www.charactercounts.org

Billy Elliot. Written by Lee Hall. Copyright © 2000 with permission of Faber & Faber.

Destiny. Written by Ann Raven, Copyright © 2006 Ann Raven. Used by permission.

"Hero." Words and music by Walter N. Afanasieff and Mariah Carey. Copyright © 1993 by Rye Songs. All rights reserved. Used by permission of Warner/Chapell Music, Inc.

"Everybody Dance." Words and music by Bernard Edwards & Nile Rodgers. Copyright © 1975 by Sony/ATV Songs LLC. All rights reserved. Used by permission of Alfred Publishing Co., Inc.

This book is dedicated to the memory of my Mom

ANDREA ADAMS

(1946 – 1995)

A pioneer who inspired a sense of justice where there was none. The legacy she left had a profound influence on my life, and through this book, will, I hope, have a powerful effect on you and your loved ones too.

Contents

Part 2: The Gift

❆❆❆❆❆❆

Part 3: In Goodbye

❊❊❊❊❊❊

Introduction

It's nice to share the gift of a kiss, a hug, a joke, or even a few fond words whenever we part. Yet sometimes we forget to express ourselves in such a caring way. Maybe we're in a hurry—rushing out the door—or perhaps there's been a disagreement, and we've parted on bad terms. But that's okay. We can pick up the phone to apologize, or share our sentiments by making amends when we meet again. It seems that we always get a second chance. Sadly, that isn't always the case. For some, the last chance comes without warning, eliminating the opportunity for a meaningful goodbye.

Just imagine what might happen if you took off for a week without having shared a loving farewell with your family. No doubt they'd be pretty disappointed and upset. Meanwhile, you'd soon realize what an idiot you'd been and call them to apologize. They would probably forgive you and it would all blow over pretty quickly. But, "what if" for some reason the *worst* were to happen, meaning that it had been your last chance to say goodbye. What then? The opportunity to tell them just how much you cared would have disappeared. Imagine how devastated your loved ones would be, knowing they'd never be able to talk to you, hug you, laugh with or see you again. That would be it. Your chance to share your love would be gone, leaving you and your surviving family in deep regret that you never took a moment to express yourself.

Despite knowing that "it" is inevitable, few of us take the time to fully prepare for the possibility of "what if." Because there's no date fixed in the diary for our final farewell, it's very easy to ignore; unless of course, the diagnosis of a terminal illness has made us acutely aware of its impending arrival. But even in such tragic circumstances typically we still brush "it" under the carpet. Otherwise we convince ourselves it's something we don't have to deal with until some time in the distant future, twenty or forty years from now. But this is a mistake. All too often "it" comes unannounced, as the result of an accident, natural disaster, sudden illness or some other terrible tragedy, and because we've ignored "it," we aren't prepared. Having done nothing to share a few fond words or leave a caring message for those who will survive us, they are left wishing there was a second chance, as they suffer in the tragedy of their loss.

In order to avoid this, it's important to ask ourselves the following questions—What would you do if you knew the exact time and date of your departure? How would you spend the remaining time? Would you share the stories of your life, the values and lessons you've learned? Would you leave a gift that your loved ones could treasure forever? Perhaps you would capture your loving thoughts in a letter, or leave something to motivate and comfort your survivors when you are no longer here. Surely, if you really knew when "it" was coming you'd do all of this, and much, much more.

By expressing yourself in these ways you can create *Your Legacy of Love* and in doing so, help those who will eventually survive you: your children, partner or lover, brother, sister and even your parents; to overcome and recover from the suffering that will be brought on by their loss. We all have the chance to reduce the impact this experience will have on our survivors and help them to cope with the challenges that are inherent to bereavement. We can begin by recognizing that tomorrow doesn't always come, and that by taking time to prepare for our final farewell we can do something to make a positive difference, and by doing so, we can all *Realize the Gift in Goodbye*.

Destiny

How long life, how long will we
Be granted to fulfill our destiny
In the vastness of the universe
Fleeting moments on earth are we
To leave our mark, make good our name
To leave cherished memories of what we became
Given freewill to make a difference
To shine like a star in its brilliance
So much to learn
So little time on our sojourn
Soon celestial angels take our hand
For the world to come, our Promised Land
Praying we leave behind a binding legacy of love
As we cross over to the heavens above

Ann Raven, 2006

PART I

****

Realize . . .

****

1

The Opportunity

The gods cannot help those who do not seize opportunities
— Chinese Proverb

I could not have written this book if my Mom were still alive, as
the insights gained from this loss would no doubt have passed me
by. I would never have understood the needs that surviving family members have to continue their connection with the person
they've lost and I'd have been incapable of appreciating the suffering that comes when someone you love so dearly dies.

Yet, this painful learning curve appears to have served a purpose,
as here I am some thirteen years on, motivated to put pen to paper and write this guide. To share what I've learned and explain
how, even in this—the saddest of goodbyes—there hides a gem,
a precious gift that each of us can realize. Unfortunately, most
of us don't discover this until it's too late. We're so afraid of the
D-Word that we don't think about preparing for the worst. We
pretend that it will never happen by hiding in denial and hoping it

will be okay. But it rarely is. For the family members and friends who will survive us, it is this exact failure to prepare for the "what if" that can make the situation so very much worse when "it" does eventually happen. Because, if we don't understand the future needs of our loved ones and haven't planned ahead for certain eventualities, then like me, they will suffer—from the immensely negative emotional and mental impact of grief. They will be left feeling confused, lonely, unloved, and unsupported. I'm sure this is something you would never want to happen. That's why I'm going to help you prepare *Your Legacy of Love*, so you can offer support to your family and friends from afar, making sure that everyone is better equipped to cope when "it"—their greatest loss—comes knocking at your door. I know it's an unpleasant thought, but just for a moment, imagine that "it" really has happened. You've departed this world and crossed to the other side. Think about the impact on your surviving family:

❈ How will they know you truly loved them?

❈ Who will share their history with them?

❈ Who will support them in their time of need?

❈ Who will comfort and care for them?

❈ How will their memories of you stay strong?

❈ Who will help them make "good" life choices?

❈ Who will motivate them when things get tough?

To Make A Difference

I know these are difficult questions that you'd probably rather not ask, but if you don't, they'll forever remain unanswered. Then, when "that" time comes, your loved ones will have to work these things out for themselves while also struggling to find solutions to the challenges inherent to bereavement. That is why it's so important to answer these questions. Not in some far off distant future— twenty or forty years from now—when you believe "it" might happen, but now, today, while you are healthy and capable of realizing this gift in goodbye.

Sadly, my Mom wasn't able to do this. She didn't have a book that explained how to minimize the suffering for her surviving loved ones, and she wasn't able to answer these questions because no one asked them. She had no idea of how important such a legacy might be for her children. If only she had been shown how to do this, I know it would have reduced some of the hurt that comes with bereavement. And I'm sure it would have helped me to achieve a far speedier and healthier recovery from my grief. But mostly, I believe it would have helped preserve the loving connection between Mom and me. That's why I am writing this book. Because I want you to know how you can comfort, guide and encourage your surviving family—even from beyond the grave—because, by recording your affections, you can help your loved ones remain connected to you long after you have gone.

In this book, I will also show you how, by using specific tools, you can reduce the mental and emotional damage that is so often caused by such a loss. It is my intention to help you prevent your loved ones from entering the *Danger Zone* or getting stuck in the *Gaping Void* of grief. I won't, however, be using academic theories. Instead, you will find that I offer hands on, how-to-make a-difference-*right-now* solutions. You'll find that Part One of this book will lead you into a deeper understanding of grief and loss, with the aim of helping you come to terms with the difficult nature of these subjects. Part Two offers a wealth of practical ideas and ways that you can easily begin to create *Your Legacy of Love*, while Part Three explores how you can become more at peace with the prospect of the end-of-life, and learn how to live the remainder of it a little more lovingly.

Because the idea for *Your Legacy of Love* was born out of personal experience—having lost my mother to cancer when I was twenty-one years old—much of this book is based on the insights I gained. Yet I have also included the thoughts, ideas and suggestions of the many survivors whom I interviewed or counseled. Some had parents who wanted to maintain a positive influence in their lives—long after they themselves had gone—so they invented ways to offer ongoing support to continue parenting by proxy. The ideas they shared are relevant not only to parents, but to anyone who wants to maintain a loving and supportive connection with their survivors—siblings, partners, parents, lovers or grandchildren—anyone who will be affected by such a loss. Before you learn how to do this, I'd like to share a little of my story so you will better understand how "it" might influence your surviving loved ones.

When "It" Happens

This all began when I was eighteen years old. Having just completed school, I'd embarked on my first independent adventure, a summer waitressing job at the Paradise Hotel on Lefkas—a magical Mediterranean island in southern Greece. The holidays quickly came to an end and it was time for me to return home to my family in England, where I spent the remaining days shepherding Jacob, my sixteen-year-old brother, and his friends on surfing trips to Bournemouth beach. For two teenagers it was a typically carefree break from the pressures of school and studies. But that was all about to change.

Mom had been to see the doctor five times that month, because even with the prescribed antibiotics her irritating cough would not subside and her Irritable Bowel Syndrome (IBS)—the apparent source of her intense stomach pains—was only getting worse. I remember coming home to find Mom and her partner

Francis comforting each other on the sofa. Their red swollen eyes and tear-stained faces gave the game away that something was up. That day she had been to see a specialist at the hospital and he'd taken tests that had resulted in a new diagnosis—secondary cancer in the lungs and liver. This was serious. Although I didn't understand the full implication of this, I did know it meant one thing—the fight was on: Mom (Andrea Adams) vs. Cancer (the Killer Disease).

This terrible news united our family with one overriding concern: could "it," might "it," would "it" happen? Then again, "it" might not. But if "it" did, then when? From the moment we learned of the prognosis, these thoughts looped roller-coaster-like in our minds, the uncertainty dictating the course of our lives. We were swept along on the winds of "what if," drifting into the place I call *Limboland*. Despite further tests, the doctors were unable to locate the primary source of the disease, which limited the chance for any successful treatment. The oncologist gave her just three months—a terribly unfair life-sentence for a forty-six-year old mother of two.

Determined that she would win the battle and wanting to protect us from this heartbreaking news, Mom and Francis kept this prognosis to themselves. They had hoped that things would stay the same, but they didn't. They changed. Suddenly our routine existence was transformed by an overwhelming supply of medications, pill bottles, boxes, syringes, tubes, and the ugly addition of a Hickman line, not to mention the endless visits to doctors, hospitals, specialists and oncologists. We had entered a strange world filled with unfamiliar faces, technology, and foreign terminology: chemotherapy, oncology, biopsy, toxicity, hematology, neutropenia, metastases, remission and relapse. The stream of friends, relatives, colleagues calling or visiting to share their good wishes or concerns was relentless. We had to adapt fast.

Yet, somehow we continued to act normally in our everyday lives. Mom continued her work as BBC radio-journalist, author, and pioneer in the campaign against *Bullying in the Workplace* as she traveled the country to provide training and consultation to Britain's leading organizations. Meanwhile Francis gave me and my brother comfort and support, leaving us free to resume our studies. However, these efforts to maintain some sense of normality were not entirely successful. There were days when the veneer cracked and the pressure of uncertainty burst through: a swiftly concealed tear when returning from the hospital, or a moment of dread when Mom winced in pain. We lived that way for two years.

Mom just wasn't prepared to accept the oncologists' terms, so she fought on, beyond the three-month prognosis, on and on. Even when the cancer was causing her agonizing pain, having spread deep into her bones, somehow she kept going. Then, on a wintry November day, the disease finally got its way, and the beautiful woman with a freckled face and cheeky grin, whose cuddles could dissolve the bitterest of tears, died peacefully at home. The "what if" had finally been resolved; "it" had come and taken away the most precious of all things: my Mom.

That was the beginning of a long and bumpy journey. I had thought that our lengthy anticipation of this loss meant that we were prepared, and this would make "it" easier to bear. But I was wrong. During those first few weeks I cried often. The feeling of despair was overwhelming. Before this, my only experience of grief amounted to the loss of Loppy the rabbit, Hoppity the hamster, and Smudge the mad Jack Russell, so grief was something I knew very little about. These pet-deaths had secured me some time off school to recover from the sadness, but really nothing more. *This* was totally different. I was shattered. I had lost my primary source of love, my beacon of light, my coach and my very best friend. It hurt. A lot. Nothing seemed to relieve that total and utter sense of loss.

Your Survivors Will Suffer

The impact "it" had on my life was immense. Even now, after the great healer Time has done its work, I find that the destructive emotions that accompany grief still challenge me even today. Feelings of loneliness, a lack of security or safety, and low self-esteem frequently creep up on me, especially during times of stress, illness, rejection or transition, when this old wound is easily torn open. Beneath the fresh scar lies a deep sorrow and regret that the person who once comforted me during such difficult times is never coming back. It's difficult to explain just how earth-shattering the experience of losing a parent can be, but I hope this entry in my diary, penned a year after Mom's death, will give you some idea:

> Kate asked me how I was doing. "Fine," I lied for the umpteenth time. What else am I meant to say? "Desperate, empty and devastated that at twenty-two-years-old I feel like a child who lost her Mommy in the supermarket, alone and scared, with no idea of the way home."

Now before you start thinking, "Surely at 22 she was old enough to cope without her Mom?" let me tell you something. When you lose the person who has provided you with care and emotional support for the majority of your life, no matter how old, how strong, or how smart you are, it will rock your world. This experience is especially challenging for children, young adults and life-long partners, particularly elderly ones. For these surviving family members, losing the person who has been their primary care-giver can be catastrophic, leaving many to suffer the negative consequences for the rest of their lives. The people who are most reliant on you will naturally have a greater need for ongoing emotional support, assistance, and guidance, if they are to have a healthy recovery. Few of us fully understand such needs, unless we have experienced the loss of a loved one first-hand. Sadly this means that many of the bereaved are left to overcome the suffering of grief all by themselves.

This was certainly the case for my brother and me. We were young adults when Mom died, so people assumed we were old enough to cope. They didn't seem to appreciate the needs we had or the challenges we faced in light of our loss. Our world had transformed from a stable and supportive place, to somewhere unsteady and foggy with grief. Mom's love—the most important ingredient in our lives, the fuel with which every mother feeds her child—had gone, and in its place was the *Gaping Void* of grief. It was a time when I should have been starting my adult life, independently carving out my own unique path. But, unlike my peers—who were making confident progress in their lives and careers—I bounced hopelessly between bewilderment and deep despair. The linchpin in my life had disappeared. The sounding board, the wise woman and maternal guide, the cheerleader who motivated me from the sidelines had gone. I felt so alone, crushed and heartbroken. I had no idea of which way to turn. Some days were okay. Others were horrible. Birthdays, holidays, anniversaries and celebrations, special days that had once been full of joy and celebration quickly became *Lonely Landmarks*. The high spirits and enthusiasm that others shared on these events only served to magnify my loss and the misery that accompanied it. The cards, cakes, presents, phone calls and cuddles were a painful reminder that the person who had been the source of these—my Mom—was no longer there.

Then there were the days when my luck had run out, my confidence had expired, or when daunting decisions presented themselves, and the struggles of everyday life—studies, exams, money, work and relationships—wore me down. Even though I tried to pick myself up and believe that things would be okay, it was the words, or arms, of my loving mother that would instantly have convinced me that all would be well. I yearned for a way to reach her, to hear some comforting words of encouragement, inspiration, or praise. Perhaps some guidance to help me choose the right path, or something to pep me up and infuse me with hope—a message that said she was "proud of me," that she "loved me" or "believed in me." Something that reminded me of how much she really cared: a note, a tape, even a few words scrawled on a napkin would have made a difference, but sadly, there was only silence.

As the years have passed, the need for a connection has faded as I have grown able and capable of relying on myself, having found solid role models from whom I can obtain the guidance I required. But this has taken me all of thirteen years and still there are days when this legacy of loss penetrates my world. I wonder about my history and how I came to be this person, questioning the stories told to me about my mother, whether they are fact or fiction. There are still moments when my heart is filled with the agony of my loss, often as the result of someone's wedding, the birth of a child, or a girlfriend announcing that they're doing something special with their Mom—something I will never again be able to do (of course, they don't realize the painful implications of such an innocent declaration).

Looking back it seems strange that although we knew Mom's death was a very real possibility, the effect it might have on us was never discussed. Not by us, nor the doctors, the nurses or the hospice workers. No one suggested that it was important to anticipate the "what if" by preparing her children, partner or family for bereavement. Nobody mentioned what she might do to help her survivors come to terms with their loss and no one explained how she might go about establishing a continuing bond of love with us. Because Mom had no prior experience of grief, it must have been really hard for her to imagine the impact that her departure would have on us. She couldn't have foreseen the struggles we would face, or have known the ways she could comfort or encourage us from afar. Because she didn't receive the kind of advice that is offered in this book, sadly, she was one of the many people who was never able to *Realize the Gift in Goodbye*.

Unless You Realize

Mom did receive some advice on preparing for her departure. She was advised to write a final Will and Testament, so that her *Financial Assets* would be distributed according to her wishes — something for which I am eternally grateful, as this was helpful both for practical and legal reasons. But this did nothing to alleviate my suffering or continue the loving bonds of our mother daughter connection. The house, car, and belongings that she passed on were of little significance in light of my loss. What I really wanted was something that reminded me of her love, especially during Christmas and birthdays, events that quickly became *Lonely Landmarks* after her death.

During the really tough times, like when I had a major car accident, was recovering from an operation, or the time I got really homesick during a work-placement in Austria, was when I yearned for some guidance or a special memento from Mom. Perhaps a letter or a card, something that shared Mom's affections and would have helped me to maintain the fading connection. I soon realized that the real value was not in her *Financial Assets* but in her *Emotional Assets* — the unique essence that made Mom who she was; her talents, the lessons she learned, the values she held, the stories of her life and the love she shared. These were the precious ingredients that formed the foundation of our relationship.

If Mom had understood how to capture and share her *Emotional Assets*, I know it would have had a powerful and positive impact on my grief. A legacy of Mom's love would have helped to prevent my connection with her from fading, while reducing my suffering, and motivating me when times were tough. I believe this would also have helped encourage a healthier recovery from my loss. As time passed and I spoke with others who had been bereaved, it became clear that my intuition was correct, as these people shared my desire for an ongoing connection to their deceased. I wanted others to understand the importance and value of our *Emotional Assets* so they could make a difference and help reduce the suffering of their survivors. But who was I to advise the world? What qualified me to make such recommendations?

I am not a psychologist and at the time had no training in grief counseling, so I began my own research. I spent four years interviewing ministers, grief counselors, hospice workers, nurses, doctors and leading experts in the fields of grief, bereavement and palliative care. I read countless articles, journals and books on grief, bereavement and related topics. I studied with CRUSE (the

UK's leading bereavement care provider) and the National Federation of Spiritual Healers (NFSH) where I also volunteered as a healer and counselor. I had spent hundreds of hours listening to the experiences of survivors who'd experienced a major loss of some kind or another. During this time, I was also awarded a Fellowship with the Winston Churchill Memorial Trust, who gave me a generous grant to explore the "Role of Love in Palliative Care." This enabled me to extend my work overseas, to the United States, where I interviewed the directors and founders of leading palliative care institutions, hospices and bereavement care centers, including the Zen Hospice in San Francisco, CA, The Dougy Center for Grieving Families and Children in Portland, OR, and the Calvary Hospital in New York, NY.

I learned a lot about the needs of the bereaved. However, I still wasn't sure that my ideas for a Legacy of Love really would be of genuine benefit to the bereaved, so I began a small independent survey, questioning people about their wishes for the legacy their parents might leave them. To my surprise, the results confirmed the desire for our *Emotional Assets*. Perhaps the strongest endorsement for this came from an elderly man, one of the few people who had received such a gift from his father, in the form of a letter that he'd written before leaving to fight in the Second World War. "I never really knew my dad. He died when I was three. But that letter has kept him in my mind and heart and will for eternity. I don't know what I'd have done without it; it's the most precious thing I own. I have to get it photo-copied, the blessed thing is in tatters I've read it so many times!"

This was the last piece in the puzzle. I finally felt that I had sufficient evidence to validate the idea that *Your Legacy of Love* would truly be of benefit to the bereaved. It was time to share what I had learned. The result is this book, where I combine and share my own insights with the ideas of the many survivors I've interviewed, so that you can learn how to prepare for the "what if" by leaving this parting gift—to keep your children, siblings, partner or lover, even parents—connected to you forevermore. As you read on, you will discover how to identify, record, and share your *Emotional Assets*, as you go about creating *Your Legacy of Love* to capture the all-important and unique essence that is *you*.

You will learn how to create *Future Surprises* combining messages, media, music, and memorabilia with tokens of your affection to inspire, uplift and remind your surviving family of how much you really cared. However, please do be warned—this might require a little bit of bravery. Not everyone can face the harsh reality of exploring their own departure. If you are already thinking "How on earth will I do this?" Then take a moment to envision your child or partner opening a letter thirty years from now. In it, you've expressed how much you're going to miss them and listed all the ways you love them, together with insights and stories about your life. Now imagine their joy when they open this treasure and realize that unlike your physical form, this heart-felt message will continue on and on.

You may still have some reservations about preparing for such an unwanted event in your life. But I can promise that this will get easier as you learn how to release your fears surrounding the *D-Word* and as you gain a better understanding of the positive impact that *Your Legacy of Love* will have on you and your loved ones. I'm convinced that when you have completed this book you'll have the guts to give this a go. Obviously you are a pioneering, courageous, kind and compassionate person—isn't that why you picked up this book in the first place? Still, if you struggle a little with some parts of this, just remember that by implementing one of the suggested ideas it will have a profound influence on your survivors' lives. Because, unlike the dozens of books that provide remedy for friends and relatives after "it" has happened, this one gives *you* the opportunity to prepare for "it" in advance—so you can *do* something to ease the suffering of your loved ones. That's why this book is about doing. Doing wonderful and inspiring things and doing them *now*, while *you* can still make a difference. Please take this opportunity to realize this gift in goodbye today, to *do* something special for your loved ones—they'll appreciate it more than you could ever imagine.

2

The Value of Emotional Assets

Never apologize for showing feeling. When you do so, you
apologize for truth — Benjamin Disraeli, Politician

When the idea for *Your Legacy of Love* first came to mind, a seed
of doubt still rattled around in my head. I didn't inherit such a
legacy from Mom, and at the time, didn't actually know anyone
who had. Despite my conviction that this would help to reduce the
mental and emotional suffering of grief, I wasn't sure if my own
needs were the same as others who had experienced such a loss.
I needed to know that this would really benefit the bereaved to
ensure I wasn't proposing something that might actually do more
harm than good. So in addition to my desk research, I started an
independent survey asking the question:

**What would you prefer if one of your parents
died: to inherit their wealth or a letter saying
how much they loved you?**

I quizzed people from all walks of life and asked them to pass this question on to their family and friends. Kindly they agreed to help, and I soon received over two hundred and fifty replies. They came from Europe, America, Canada, Asia and Australia, with responses from business people, parents, children, professionals, servicemen and women, doctors, lawyers, homemakers, artists, musicians and engineers—the majority of whom had already lost someone close to them.

Why Meaningful Words Win Over Money

It was a relief to discover that I wasn't alone. Over ninety percent of these people expressed a wish to have some words preserved on paper. Of the tiny minority who didn't want a letter, one woman joked that if there was a chance she might inherit a château in the south of France, she would have to take it (there's always one!). Perhaps she never saw the film *Billy Elliot*—which illustrates the power of a simple message for surviving family members. *Billy Elliot* is the story of a young boy growing up in the north of England during the miners' strikes of the early '80s. He struggles to cope with the loss of his mother and to deal with his father's grief at having lost both his wife and his job. Unknown to Billy, his mother wrote him a letter before she died, leaving instructions for it to be presented to him on his eighteenth birthday. Concerned about him and his behavior, his Grandmother prematurely delivers the gift, hoping it will encourage his recovery. Billy is just eleven when he receives his mother's letter:

To My Son Billy,

I know that I must seem like a distant memory to you, which is probably a good thing. It will have been a long time and I will have missed seeing you grow, missed you crying, laughing and shouting and I will have missed telling you off. But please know that I was always there with you, through everything, and I always will be. I am proud to have known you, and I am proud that you were mine.

Always be yourself, I love you forever.

Mom

These kind and encouraging words have a potent effect on young Billy. The support and appreciation he receives from his mother through this letter seems to give him the strength to fight the cultural and familial battles that prevented him from pursuing his passion for ballet, the only thing he loves. He shares the precious letter with his dance teacher, Mrs.Wilkinson, the one person who seems to believe in him. Moved by what she reads, Mrs.Wilkinson begins helping Billy to develop his talent for dancing, while encouraging him to do something he would never otherwise have dreamed of: to audition for the Royal School of Ballet in London where he eventually performs as a dancer.

Billy's mom was not alone in understanding the power that meaningful words could have for her surviving offspring. The majority of people who responded to my survey were very clear about their desire for a legacy that preserved the loving words of their parents so that, in their absence, these special sentiments could be enjoyed over and over again. However, this isn't what we're traditionally encouraged to do. Normally, lawyers and financial advisors who give us information on preparing for the "what if" suggest that we write a Will in order to record the instructions for the distribution of our *Financial Assets*.

This is extremely important, because, if the worst does happen and you have ignored this advice, your *Financial Assets* will be deemed "intestate" which means that the probate court will appoint an administrator to distribute your assets according to state law. Generally the rules are pretty fair and in time your estate will be passed to your spouse, children or your next of kin. Probate is a lengthy process that can drag on for months, even years, during which time your assets are inaccessible to your surviving family, which can cause untold amounts of unnecessary stress, especially if they are unable to support themselves financially during this time. Adding insult to injury, a much higher percentage of your *Financial Assets* will also be eaten up in taxes.

Writing a Will is an essential element of preparing for the "what if," yet more as a practicality to protect your loved ones, as it fails to account for your *Total Wealth*, ignoring the immense value that exists in your *Emotional Assets*. Despite the common belief that money and material possessions are all that matter, when the life of someone dear has been lost, the value of your *Financial Assets* will depreciate rapidly. Your house, cash, company or car might appear to be the most important elements of your legacy, but in truth, these *things* will be of less significance to your survivors when your love and affection have been lost forever.

What Matters Most

In the course of my research I found that it is our *Emotional Assets* that matter most to our survivors. One ground-breaking study identified that the majority considered non-financial leave-behinds to be ten times more important than the financial aspects of a legacy. *The Allianz American Legacies Study* was commissioned by the Allianz Life Insurance Company and Age Wave to assess the preferences of 2,670 baby boomers (people born between 1946 and 1964) and their elderly parents, regarding the practical issues of legacies. "Many people wrongly assume the most important issue among families is money and wealth transfer, it's not," said President of Age Wave, Ken Dychtwald. He went on to say, "This national survey found that for the overwhelming majority, legacy transfer has to do with deeper, more emotional issues. An inheritance focuses primarily on the money, but a true legacy also includes memories, lessons and values you teach to your children over a lifetime."

This study was a key piece of research, providing overwhelming evidence that the desire for a legacy combining *Emotional Assets* with the more traditional aspects is in fact widespread. Although my own study was much smaller, I had obtained detailed information about people's personal preferences for a non-financial legacy. Many of the people I interviewed said they wanted a piece of memorabilia, something to keep alive the memories of their dearly departed. Some suggested it would be helpful to have a gift to open on special days, like Christmas or a birthday. One thirty-year-old man, whom we'll call Matthew, said he'd like to inherit the football shirt his father had worn to the games they'd attended. Matthew believed it would remind him of the fun they'd had; helping him to recall the cheeky humor his Dad had expressed so freely during the games. Suzy, an elderly woman, wrote to say that if she could inherit one thing she'd choose her mother's apron as it would remind her of all the times happily spent cooking family meals together. Sarah, a young teenager, said she'd want the diaries her Mom had written every year since she was born, knowing that these contained the stories and secrets of both her mother's life and her own. Matthew, Suzy and Sarah's requests are very common. Although these everyday items may seem of little value, when you've lost the person you love, such seemingly unimportant things become priceless.

Despite the evidence confirming this universal desire for *Emotional Assets*, I have only encountered a few who received such a loving legacy or were thoughtful enough to create one. Yet it seems that the propensity to gift our values, rather than our valuables, is increasing. Journalist Lizette Alvarez observes this trend in her 2005 *New York Times* article, *Farewell with Love and Instructions*: "Hoping to nurture their children from afar and assuage the dread of leaving a child too soon, a small but growing number of terminally ill parents are painstakingly leaving behind more tangible links: audiotapes, videos, letters, cards and gifts that children can use to bolster memories and use as a guiding hand. The tapes bear messages of love and remembrance: the dress a daughter wore on her first day of kindergarten, the thrill of a trip to Yankee Stadium, a son's jitters before a first piano recital. The letters riff on parents' life stories, their hopes for their children and the life lessons they wish to impart. Some parents choose gifts or cards for future birthdays or Christmas celebrations. One mother created a tape to be given to her son on his wedding day, if and when that occasion arrives. One father left written messages behind paintings, a surprise that his children stumbled across a year after his death. Through these things, dying parents bequeath courage, laughter, a semblance of companionship and even a guiding hand. The keepsakes help crowd out the searing tableaux of death with reminders of how Mom or Dad sounded, moved and thought about life …"

When I first read this article, my immediate reaction was delight. "Brilliant!" I thought, "People *are* doing this and making a difference." But then I wondered, "Why hadn't Mom done this?" She was proactive, imaginative, open minded, loving, and cared about us deeply. She had all the qualities of someone who'd be inspired to leave a Legacy of Love. After giving this considerable thought, I came to the conclusion that various factors were at play. Mom had no awareness of *Emotional Assets* or the inherent value these would have for her children. No one had explained how powerful this would be, and there were no books or articles describing the long-term benefits of such a thing. I'm sure she gave some thought to sharing her stories or writing a letter to convey a loving message, but I know how scared she was of acknowledging that "it" was lurking just around the corner, and this prevented her from taking action. According to Dr. William Breitbart, Chief of Psychiatry at New York's Memorial Sloan Kettering Cancer Center, this reaction is quite common. Commenting in Lizette Alvarez's *New York Times* article, he explains, "It's profoundly beneficial for the kids. But it is rare. Almost everyone thinks about it, but it will get delayed or put off. I think it's very difficult to do this because it really demands a confrontation, an admission, a real admission that you are dying, and that is very hard for most people. What is at play is this struggle in their mind between hope and despair. It takes on such incredible significance, a final message, it has to be said perfectly."

Preserving the Connection

But there are no perfect words to share when someone has passed away, just as there is no one-size-fits-all formula for creating Your Legacy of Love. The general themes already mentioned—your stories, values and memories, your guidance and support—will be of significant benefit to anyone surviving a loss, especially to younger children, including nieces, nephews and grandchildren, who will benefit from your wisdom regarding key life issues such as religion, relationships, growing up, sexuality, career, education and love. The film *My Life* is a great illustration of how to go about passing on this knowledge. Made in the early '90s, this film portrays the story of happily married couple Bob (Michael Keaton) and Gail (Nicole Kidman) who are expecting their first child, when sadly they discover that Bob has cancer and may have only four months to live. Consequently they must face the fact that Bob may never meet his own son. In light of this news, Bob decides to make a film about his life with the aim of teaching his son everything that a parent should.

He begins by sharing the details of his ancestry, filming a collection of family memorabilia (including his own baby pictures), a painting of his tiny infant footprints and family photos, then he interviews friends and colleagues who share anecdotes about the kind of man he is. Bob then films himself conducting the all-important "how-to" aspects of a man's life—cooking spaghetti, playing basketball, shaving, entering a room, giving a good handshake and jump-starting a car! Finally, in an attempt to create the scenario of a father-to-son chat, Bob faces the camera and talks to his son about sex and music, explaining, "Your mother would be little help on these subjects. There are some things that have to be told straight, man to man." Bob then relays the story of how he and Gail met and fell in love, explaining that one day Gail might meet another man, possibly even remarry. Concluding his parting gift, Bob shares some selfless advice on this matter by gently advising his son that this might make him feel very angry or possibly, if he likes the new man, leave him feeling that he is being disloyal. On this delicate subject, Bob tells his son, "I will not be jealous. It will make me very happy for Gail to meet another man. I will always be your real father, and I will live on through you. I love you." The film is kept in a safe place, until the time comes when their son is old enough to understand and Gail can deliver the precious gift to him.

The *My Life* scenario shows how little more than a good dose of imagination is required to capture your *Emotional Assets* and share them through *Your Legacy of Love*. This film also touches on some of the issues your survivors might encounter, giving a good example of how to deal with the idea of being "replaced" as a lover, spouse, or parent. Although this may make you rather uncomfortable, it's important to realize that such issues will affect your loved ones and that by recording your thoughts and views on these subjects, you can help clear things up in advance so your survivors aren't left wondering and worrying for the rest of their lives. Although its important to keep in mind that what you say in *Your Legacy of Love* could have a negative effect on survivors —especially young ones—and to remember that this is not an exercise in blackmail from the beyond!

The Bonus: You Get Peace of Mind

As you embark on this journey of creating *Your Legacy of Love*, you'll soon discover why therapists have been supporting the idea of a more meaningful legacy for quite some time. Research has shown that when patients share their emotions or leave meaningful objects through what is often referred to as a "Heart Will" or "Dignity Therapy," that it makes a significant difference to their mental and emotional well-being. In recent years these concepts have generated considerable interest and support among the care community, resulting in an international clinical study into "Dignity Therapy." Led by Dr. Harvey Chochinov, director of the Manitoba Palliative Care Research Unit, this trial focused on one hundred terminally ill patients who were interviewed by a therapist:

"Tell me a little about your life history, particularly the parts you either remember most or things that were most important."

These often highly emotional discussions were recorded, capturing the information so that it could later be shared with the patients' family members and friends. Participants were encouraged to find an appropriate ending that conveyed a poignant message to their loved ones. One participant, a thirty-six-year-old woman with breast cancer noted, "I'm very happy to have participated in this project. It's helped bring my memories, thoughts, and feelings into perspective, instead of all jumbled emotions running through my head. The most important thing has been that I'm able to leave a sort of 'insight' of myself for my husband, and children, and all my family, and friends." The results of this study, which were published in the *Journal of Clinical Oncology*, showed significant benefits for both patients and their families:

91% reported a satisfaction with "Dignity Therapy"
81% felt it had or would be of help to their family
67% said it gave their life meaning

Dr. Chochinov remarked on the positive influence "Dignity Therapy" could have in significantly reducing suffering and depression for people preparing for the end-of-life. "It is noteworthy that patients who felt that the intervention had or might have some benefit for their family were most likely to report a heightened sense of meaning and purpose, along with a lessening of suffering. For dying patients, the salutary effects of safeguarding the well-being of those they are about to leave behind seems to extend to the end-of-life itself." Yet even with the promise of such a positive outcome, the idea of creating *Your Legacy of Love* might still be rather daunting. According to Dr. Donna Schuurman, Director of the Dougy Center for Grieving Children and Families, that is because, "In our largely death-denying society we have a culture that values 'moving on' rather than 'remembering'. People just don't know how to do it."

This concept is still relatively new for everyone, so it's common to be unsure and a little afraid at this stage. Whether you are the picture of perfect health, or facing your worst nightmare (with only a little time to spare), preparing *Your Legacy of Love* might appear a little challenging. I imagine that Billy's mother shed more than a few tears when penning that heartfelt letter, and the chances are you will too. Realizing your *Emotional Assets* certainly requires courage, determination and a good dose of imagination. But, remember, the gift of your love has numerous benefits for you, your surviving family, their family and the generations who are still to come. They are relying on you to help them in their time of need, to leave a reminder of who you were and how much you cared. You might find this exercise difficult at times, but please don't give up or let your loved ones down. No one knows when "that" time is going to come, so please take this opportunity to *Realize the Gift in Goodbye* and consider the words of Pablo Picasso: "Only put off until tomorrow what you are willing to die having left undone."

3

Getting to Grips with Grief

Blessed are those who mourn, for they shall
be comforted — Matthew 5:4

You may be wondering, if your *Emotional Assets* are so valuable,
why you haven't heard of them before, and why isn't everyone
capturing them? There are actually a variety of reasons behind
why most people aren't leaving non-financial legacies, which
originate from the changes—in cultural, professional and historical attitudes—towards death and bereavement, that have occurred
in the past century. Collectively, these attitudinal shifts have pro-
moted our denial of the *D-Word* and conspired to prevent us from
getting to grips with grief.

Until relatively recently, it was extremely common to pass on a
non-financial legacy because of a shared a belief in the after-life,
which motivated people to leave gifts that would maintain the
connection between the living and their dearly departed. It was
considered perfectly natural and normal to leave all manner of
objects (which had some perceived traditional or religious mean-

ing), as part of an inheritance. The Victorians gave lockets of hair, which their bereaved typically wore in a piece of jewelry, while South American tribes bequeathed bones for survivors to wear in their hair!

The Madness of the "Must Move On" March

These traditions began to change at the beginning of the twentieth century, as the advances in science and medicine began to alter people's attitudes about many things, including the existence of the afterlife. Rationalization became the order of the day. People began demanding proof as the medical field progressed in both technology and skill, together with our expectation for longevity. This meant that death—previously viewed as a natural and in-evitable process—was suddenly perceived as a failure of modern medicine.

Behaviors and beliefs changed, shifting from a desire for a con-nection with the deceased to one an attitude of dread and disasso-ciation. Not only amongst the general public, but also within the psychological community, who began adopting the belief that it was unhealthy for survivors to maintain links with their dearly de-parted. Therapists began claiming that this would promote delu-sions about the afterlife, hinder healing and prevent patients from moving on. The emphasis changed from *remembering* to *removing* as psychologists, psychiatrists, and counselors began marching to the beat of *Must Move On*. This mantra is something you may have witnessed personally when someone you love passed on. In the aftermath of this tragic event you may have been advised to "Stop crying; it will only upset everyone," or been told "Don't worry, you'll get over it soon." Alternatively, after some time passed, someone may have offered one of the classic *Must Move On* tenets, such as "It's been a year, you should have forgotten about them now," or "Come out tonight, it's time you moved on," or maybe they were callous enough to say, "Must you always talk about him or her? They aren't coming back, you know."

Although these comments may seem shocking, sadly, they are not uncommon. Just imagine how you'd feel if you received this kind of sympathy after you'd lost the person who had been central to your happiness for the past twenty, thirty, even sixty years; someone with whom you'd shared lessons, laughter, intimacy, arguments and even your deepest darkest secrets. It's hardly comforting to be told to "hurry up," "quick march" or "move along," as if you're running late for a busy commuter train. Unfortunately, this is the effect that the *Must Move On* mantra has had on our society and sadly it has spread way beyond the psychological community. The idea of wiping away the memories of your relationship to someone special seems a little strange to me, especially at a time when the bereaved naturally want to remember every little detail, to cling to the last remnants of the person who meant so much to them. You see, the problem with this modern mantra is that grief doesn't have a predetermined arrival and departure schedule like the 9:05 train from Grand Central. Although, I guess it's no great surprise when you look at our fast-paced and forward-focused world: a place where calm, time-consuming activities like reflecting and reminiscing appear to be so very old school. But, I can tell you that this "get over it" approach is not only confusing and unhealthy, it's also contrary to the real needs of the bereaved. This widespread acceptance of the *Must Move On* mantra has actually been very damaging, leaving behind many casualties with deep and painful wounds.

I know this because I have counseled many survivors, who, because of the influence of the *Must Move On* mantra, have buried or bottled up their thoughts and feelings. As a result, they experienced a lot of unnecessary pain and suffering. It's quite easy to spot them. They usually display some very obvious symptoms: they're uptight, never talk about *him* or *her* and are emotionally constipated, unable to express what they feel for fear of the mess when everything they've been withholding comes bursting out. They are often edgy and tired due to the tension that comes from restraining their feelings, which can leave them in a state of total exhaustion, barely surviving. The emotional toxicity caused by this suppression can be extremely dangerous for both the physical and mental health of the bereaved.

It was easy for me to spot these people because for many years I suffered like this too. I knew that despite having been persuaded by counselors, friends, or family members, that they *Must Move On* and forget about their departed loved ones, secretly wished they could share their memories or talk with someone who understood their sense of loss. That's why, when I gave them a little encouragement that "it's good to remember," the tears finally flowed and often I witnessed years of anguish wash away. For many, this was the first time they were able to feel that having a memory of their mom, dad, brother or sister was indeed okay.

For me, the *Must Move On* mantra began to take effect just a few months after Mom died. During the days that immediately followed her death (when it seemed acceptable to remember), I sat around with family members and friends happily reminiscing about the wonderful, funny, memorable times we'd all spent with her. Throughout the first few months there was a steady stream of well-wishers, sympathy cards and empathetic calls. Even when I returned to college to continue my studies, I found that my good friends were mostly supportive of my situation, but after a few weeks, something strange began to happen. People started calling to say, "You must stop moping and come out to play," others suggested, "Focus on your studies, it's your future, that's what's important now." These amateur psychologists thought they knew what was best; but they didn't. I wasn't even close to coming to terms with my loss. In fact, the reality and depth of losing my mother was only just beginning to sink in. I was suffering a total state of bewilderment, as my diary entry from the time shows:

> I have no idea when I fell asleep last night, sometime in between the sobs I guess. I awoke this morning feeling destroyed. The hours of crying have completely drained me, I slept for 12 hours, but still I am exhausted. The pain is unbearable, I had no idea that anything could hurt this much. I don't know that I will ever feel happy and normal again.

The contradiction between my needs and the opinions of others only worsened over time. When I tried to talk openly about my feelings, people clammed up, turned on the TV, or changed the subject. Some stopped calling while others, to my great horror, pretended not to notice me when they saw me walking down the road, and some even crossed to the other side of the street! But it didn't stop there. When visiting a good friend, I noticed that some photographs of Mom they'd once proudly displayed were no longer to be seen. It all seemed very strange. I couldn't understand why people were acting as if Mom had never existed. I was young, confused and disturbed by this behavior, but I didn't know what else to do, so I went along with it. I didn't realize that these people were actually scared, embarrassed or uncertain of what to say. I had no idea that they'd been brainwashed by the *Must Move On* motto, so I did what seemed to be expected of me and joined in the façade.

The Gaping Void You Want Them to Avoid

I began maintaining the pretense that all was well, even though this exhausted me. I had all of these wonderful memories, stories and moments that I'd shared with this great woman, yet I could no longer speak of them, so I retreated inside. This, of course, only left me feeling more separated, isolated and ignored than before. I had no one to share my suffering with, and nowhere to go, apart from the secret world of my diary, which seemed to be the only safe place to express my pain:

> Today I sat at the back of the lecture room to avoid all the stares. Since I came back, every-one treats me differently, they look at me in strange ways and conversations are hushed when I walk by. Halfway through the lecture, the pain came rushing back. Those bitter tears welled in my eyes, and that agony flooded my heart. I wanted to scream. But I couldn't break down, not in front of them.

It took all my strength but somehow I swallowed the pain, held back the tears and put my eyes to the ground. I have no recollection of what the lecturer said, but what matters is that I managed to contain myself until the end of class.

In their excellent *Grief Recovery Handbook*, John W. James and Russell Friedman describe this as "Academy Award Behavior." It's a classic outcome of the *Must Move On* approach, which leaves survivors acting as if they're okay when really they're not. When asked about their loss, the bereaved will often respond with statements designed to project a false image of recovery, such as, "I'm fine," or "Don't worry about me, it's my dad you should be concerned about." They do this so as not to burden others with their feelings, to prevent criticism or judgment, and to stop the scary emotions they are withholding from escaping.

Unfortunately, this Oscar-winning behavior only increases the sense of suffering and isolation for survivors. This habit of rationalizing and reasoning emotions or shutting off feelings is dangerous, and if encouraged, can cause considerable emotional, physical and mental damage, driving the bereaved towards what I call the *Gaping Void*, or what is commonly recognized as the *Danger Zone* of grief.

Obviously, we don't want this to happen to your survivors. That's why it's important for you to understand how your family can have a healthy recovery from their grief. Rather than living by the *Must Move On* mantra, you can help them remain connected to you, and teach them how to openly express and release their feelings so they won't end up in the *Danger Zone*. Through *Your Legacy of Love* you can give them tools to help them cope with their grief, and to encourage their healing by helping them recall memories and motivating positive moods. With this continuing bond, they will naturally, in their own time, overcome their grief and slowly assimilate their loss.

For me, this natural acceptance took a lot longer than necessary. This was partly because I didn't receive any guidance from health care professionals, which left me unprepared to deal with my loss, but also because I didn't feel as though I could ask for help. Instead, I just kept quiet and soldiered on. There were many Oscar-winning performances to project the impression that I was doing okay. Really, I had just buried myself in my work and was pretended everything was fine, suppressing all the emotions of my grief. I compartmentalized my feelings by squeezing them deep into the recesses of my body and mind. The only available space was in my heart, where the absence of my mother's love had left a hole—a gaping void. I blocked all thoughts of the woman who had been the center of my world for twenty-one years and eleven months. It was extremely uncomfortable, unnatural even, and I now realize, totally unnecessary. As a result, I was stressed, edgy and worn out. I found a way to numb the pain by filling the void with a diet of drugs, shopping, and fake friends—it seemed to work. Everyone began congratulating me: "How great, you seem to be coping so well," or "Look at how quickly you have moved on!" I think for a while I even had myself fooled, except at night when the pretense melted away as I buried my tear-stained face in the comfort of my boyfriend's arms. Now, I'm a little savvier in matters relating to grief. I understand that this was not the way to integrate or recover from my loss. More to the point, I know for sure that the *Must Move On* approach doesn't work. It only encourages disassociation and denial while promoting damaging and destructive behaviors—warning signs that would scream DANGER to the trained eye.

I somehow survived in this state for almost two years, but as with all illusions, the bubble eventually had to burst; I had a meltdown. My extremely concerned family sent me off to see a grief counselor. Exhausted by the façade I'd been living, I happily complied. During the weekly hour-long sessions, I was rarely asked a single question about my Mom, other than when and how she died. Instead I was advised to remove all reminders of her from my life, take down pictures, destroy letters, remove her belongings and focus on the future—"How would I go about forming new relationships and develop my life and career?" The conversation was all one way. I was expected to talk, the counselor to listen. If I had nothing to say, we sat there in silence, staring blankly at each other. Leaving me wondering why I had bothered to leave work early, traveling halfway across London, just so that we could sit in silence or note my apparent progress (or lack of it), which seemed to be nothing more than a numb butt, and a deeper state of depression!

The Badge of Bereavement

Once again, the *Must Move On* mantra had come to haunt me. All I really wanted was to talk to someone and share what I missed about my Mom, to tell them that I yearned for a tangible reminder of her love, and explain how difficult life seemed without her. After six months, when things hadn't improved, I decided to ditch the silent counseling sessions and started taking Prozac instead. Needless to say, the cocktail of anti-depressants and recreational drugs that I used to self-medicate probably wasn't the best solution! But it seemed to work, if only temporarily. It got me through my final year of college and I graduated with flying colors— which I must confess was the only positive result of using drugs and burying myself in work.

Then, it was time to leave the security of the college campus, my good friends, and the comforting arms of my wonderful boyfriend. This was the first major transition I had made since my loss, and it should have been the beginning of a new and exciting journey, but I was scared. Mom wasn't there to give me advice on this new phase of life. She couldn't share her wisdom, words of encouragement or faith in me—the very things I needed to help me trust that I could make it on my own. I wished she had left me some instructions, a "How-to" guide, or even better, a letter scribed with her familiar and supportive words: "Darling, it's okay, remember that I will always believe in you." I became truly conscious, perhaps for the first time, that Mom wasn't going to share in my struggles or successes, or watch her daughter grow into a woman, a wife, and one day a mother. She could no longer support me, guide me, or light the way. I felt completely lost and alone, and with this realization, I fell deeper into the *Gaping Void*.

What on earth was I supposed to do? I knew I couldn't carry on this way, with my feelings all locked up, burdened by the baggage of my pent-up grief. Despite finding a job, my life remained a mess. I was always seeking to replace my mother's love, mostly with the attention of some random guy. I was drinking and taking drugs, although I did give up the Prozac, and I had thrown myself into work as a means of escape. Initially, the crazy hours I worked earned many compliments for my commitment, but as time wore on, I started struggling—I had to drag myself out of bed each day and was often late for work. I went through the motions but nothing felt real and I was barely scraping through the day. It seemed that my highly developed talent for pretending that everything was okay had landed me in a hole, and I couldn't seem to dig my way out.

By now, it was apparent to everyone that my attempts to "move on" were only taking me round in circles. I decided the only solution was to take matters into my own hands. Instead of self-medicating, I began self-educating; reading and listening to anything I could find on grief and bereavement. However, all the advice seemed to encourage the *Must Move On* approach, and I had already learned that this wasn't bringing me any closer to a healthy recovery. So I took some time out for reflection. My first epiphany was the realization that despite commonly being referred to as the same thing, grief and bereavement are two entirely different experiences.

While grief doesn't necessarily involve bereavement, bereavement always involves grief, because grief is a temporary emotional response to a change in circumstance, or the loss of something, whereas bereavement is permanent. Grief is actually something we experience on a regular basis whenever there is a change in our circumstances. However, the severity of our grief and the consequent impact on our mental, emotional, and physical well-being varies, according to the degree of change that has occurred, and the relative level of attachment we had to the former condition or person. For example, if we have a purse or wallet stolen, the natural response is a sense of loss, but it will probably only last for a few hours or a couple of days. When we move, or lose a home, perhaps because of a fire, flood or divorce, the resulting grief will last longer. It takes time to rebuild a sense of familiarity and security, to settle into a new place and way of life. During this grieving period we may have all sorts of inexplicable feelings; anger, sadness, apathy and depression. Inevitably, there will be a sense of longing for how things used to be, yet because the thing that we lost can be replaced, these feelings usually pass as we adjust to our new possessions or surroundings, and begin to form new experiences and memories. If only this were the case for the bereaved.

Bereavement is not a temporary experience. The loss of a living, laughing, loving human being or animal is permanent. No one can ever replace the person or pet we have lost. This can be an extremely difficult thing to accept, especially when "it" happens unexpectedly, or there wasn't a chance to say goodbye. In the early stages, the bereaved commonly find that they are on an emotional roller coaster ride, oscillating between states of feeling "normal" and feeling "destroyed," sometimes within a matter of hours. Everything in their world has changed; their regular and routine existence has been turned into a topsy-turvy mess. The scale of grief experienced by the bereaved is different for everyone, and will depend on how the loss occurred, the health and ages of the survivors, and their relationship to the person who passed on. Yet, because bereavement specifically relates to death, even after the devastating feelings of grief have faded, the sense of having lost something vital, and the effect this has on survivors, continues on. It can take many years to integrate the death of a loved one, while others never come to terms with such a life-changing event. Bereavement is unending, it becomes your identity; an unwelcome label that leaves you sticking out in a crowd.

Our collective understanding of grief and bereavement was born from the work of Swiss-born psychiatrist Dr. Elisabeth Kübler-Ross. During the '60s, Dr. Kübler Ross interviewed patients at College of Chicago Billings Hospital who had been diagnosed with a terminal illness. Noting their emotional response to this tragic news, she found some commonalities in their experiences, which she referred to as the five stages: Denial, Anger, Bargaining, Depression and Acceptance. Because little other research had been conducted into grief or bereavement at that time, this study became known as the *Five Stages* model of grief and was quickly adopted by psychologists, counselors, nurses, the clergy and caregivers as a way of interpreting and helping people to "complete" their grieving. It wasn't until the '80s that more thorough investigations of the impacts of grief emerged, suggesting that the *Five Stages* model didn't really apply to people grieving the loss of a loved one at all.

Remember Me with Continuing Bonds

The ground-breaking work of Dr. Kübler-Ross raised considerable awareness of a subject where previously there was none. However, the application of this model from terminally ill patients to the bereaved has caused an awful lot of confusion, and perhaps planted the seed for the rather damaging *Must Move On* model. Fortunately, during the early '90s a new concept surrounding the experience of bereavement emerged, challenging the previously upheld belief that "moving on" was essential. Extensive research conducted by twenty-two authors (among the most respected in their fields), concluded that the popular *Must Move On* model wasn't just breaking ties, but also hearts and lives—something that bereaved families had known for years.

These findings, presented in the book *Continuing Bonds: New Understandings of Grief*, showed that despite cultural and professional objections, survivors were maintaining links or continuing bonds with their departed. Far from being in denial or some kind of pathological state—as was the common understanding—this ongoing connection provided a source of great comfort and solace, enabling the bereaved to find a healthy and natural resolution to their grief. After the introduction of this concept, the bereavement care and psychological communities began to recognize that a more comprehensive model of bereavement was needed. Dr. Gloria Horsley, renowned family therapist and National Board

Member of America's leading grief support organization, Compassionate Friends, is a keen advocate of the need for *Continuing Bonds*. She speaks from personal experience, having lost her son, Scott, at the tender age of seventeen in a car accident.

Together with her daughter, Dr. Heidi Horsley, who co-hosts the radio show *Healing the Grieving Heart of America* and teaches several courses in grief and loss as an adjunct professor at Columbia University School of Social Work, they talk about their desire for an ongoing connection to Scott, even though everyone told them to "let go". "Well-meaning people told us we would eventually 'move on with our lives,' 'get over it,' or 'find closure.' These concepts were not confirming and did not make sense to us. We didn't want to 'get-over' Scott. To 'get over' him felt somehow like we were erasing him from our lives. Scott is the only son and brother we will ever have, and we don't want to eliminate our relationships with him. To deny them would be to deny an important part of ourselves. Yes, the pain has substantially decreased over the years, but our connections remain strong."

Thankfully, a major shift is now taking place in the way people are educated, informed and counseled about grief and bereavement. "Rather than cutting ties, we are now given permission and even encouraged to maintain emotional bonds," says Dr. Gloria Horsley. Still, many people are left to figure this out for themselves. It took me ten painful years to realize that what my intuition had been telling me was actually the healthier way to go about recovering from my loss. It wasn't until the tenth anniversary of Mom's death that I made the decision that ten years was too long; it was time to listen to my intuition and start a new chapter. Rather than the usual pretending, I tentatively began to share memories with friends and reminisce with family members about the times spent with Mom. It wasn't easy at first, as I had to reverse everything that I'd learned to do during those ten long years. Thankfully, my mother is now very much present in my life. Her photo sits proudly by my bed, and I love sharing stories of our time together. Although, this didn't happen overnight; it was a slow and often distressing experience, as the bonds that I had tried so very hard to bury, slowly unwound. But it certainly wasn't nearly as painful as being told to "cut all ties" and "move on."

I hope that you are now beginning to see just how important Your Legacy of Love will be for your survivors, and how this can prevent them from being swayed by the *Must Move-On* mantra. When you leave them this *Continuing Bond*—your stories, values or morals, and an expression of your love—you keep them connected to you and the memories of the times you spent together, which will bring them great comfort in their time of distress.

4

Don't Mention the D-Word!

Death when unmasked shows us a friendly face and is a terror only at a distance — Oliver Goldsmith, Playwright

Imagine the worst has happened. You are standing at the Great Pearly Gates but you can't go in. You're looking down onto the scene below: your grieving loved ones are sitting at your bedside, distraught, devastated and empty-handed. You'd read this book and thought, "Wow! This is such a great idea. I have the opportunity to do something special, to make a lasting difference for my family. This is so important, I must find some time to start my Legacy of Love this weekend," but unfortunately that never happened. Now you must witness their pain and suffering without being able to do a thing about it. This isn't what you wanted. How on earth did you make such a mistake? If only you had taken action, just five short minutes to put yourself in their shoes, or a few hours to share your precious *Emotional Assets*. You start to realize that you didn't have to do it all—by creating just one element of Your Legacy of Love you would have made a real difference. Now it's a lost cause.

If you're not affected by this image, then stop here. However, if this passage gives you butterflies, or makes your gut drop through the floor, then I'm guessing you're someone with a lot of love to give. Only there's probably something stopping you. Most likely, you are experiencing a common disease, otherwise known as denial of the *D-Word*! It's a major barrier to helping your loved ones from afar, and the stumbling block that can stop you from taking the action necessary to create Your Legacy of Love. That's why we're going to look deeper into this disease, so you will know how to spot the symptoms and understand how to treat them, leaving you free to take action that will make a positive difference in your survivors' lives.

A Diagnosis of Denial: What's Stopping You?

In the Western world, we "immortal souls" are completely disassociated, yet secretly captivated by the *D-Word*. We live in a death-denying, death-defying society. Mention "it" during dinner and your fellow diners will swiftly steer the discussion to a more appetizing topic. Apart from those who work in the caring professions, "it" remains one of our few taboos. Commonly, "it" is considered morbid, depressing, superstitious, and dark, yet secretly we find it fascinating. Notice how people rubberneck when passing a road accident, or gawk at news reports of murders, shootings, acts of terrorism, abductions and natural disasters. Not to mention the millions we spend to watch the slaughter of a bunch of innocents in grizzly horror films each year. However, this curiosity seems to be something we are only comfortable indulging at a distance. We enjoy watching because "it" is happening to *them,* not *us.* We're perfectly happy to explore this from the safety of our cars, sofas or cinema seats, but to consider what will happen when "it" happens to us—to explore the potential impact of the "what if"—is something most of us will do almost anything to avoid.

It appears that various forces conspire to keep our heads buried ostrich-like in the sand, beginning with the multi-billion dollar beauty industry, whose repetitive broadcast of the "youth is power" message has led us to repel the idea of getting old. Consequently, we're prepared to suffer the painful price and slice of the plastic surgeon's knife, or subject ourselves to endless skin scrapes, peels and injections, in an attempt to stay beautiful and youthful forever. We think nothing of spending a few hundred dollars on a single anti-aging product. In fact, we'll try anything—creams and lotions, miracle vitamin combinations, and mysterious health potions—so long as there is a promise of vitality and longevity. (Although I'm convinced that our consumption of these wonder-treatments does little more than put a sparkle in the eyes of their company shareholders!)

Yet our inability to mention "that" word isn't entirely due to the powerful persuasion of the powder-puff providers. There is another industry responsible for fueling this denial, an industry with cover-up artists whose cosmetic skills rival those of the beauty industry. Safely hidden behind closed doors, they busy themselves cleaning, preserving, manicuring and manipulating to erase all signs of aging and the reason for demise. Having concealed all consequences of the *D-Word*, the survivors are then allowed to see the tidy, pretty, perfect body. In principle, this seems like a good idea. But this temporary measure, to make things look a little better, is like sweeping dirt under the rug in preparation for a visiting relative — it doesn't necessarily fool or delight everyone.

Science has also contributed to this denial with the invention of cryogenic suspension. It works by slowly cooling the body to freezing temperatures, temporarily suspending human life. This means that those in possession of a fat check book (cryopreservation costs thousands) have the option to re-schedule their appointment with the Grim Reaper. Since the first case in 1976 a thousand or so people have been put on ice, convinced that after a cold spell on "pause," they can extend their shelf life. However, scientists are yet to find the "play" button required to restore these frozen beauties back to life. Even if they do, you have to wonder if they'll end up like Woody Allen, who in the film *Sleeper,* is woken some two hundred years in the future with a bill for 2,400 months of rent!

You see, the problem is that we're terrified of what's around the corner. The journey we inevitably take doesn't lead to a familiar place; instead, the train we must all board, departs for Destination Unknown. A place where some cheery theorists claim we'll encounter the divine wrath of a deity, or find an empty void into which we simply disappear. Others believe that when we cross to the other side, our earthly actions will be judged and we will be punished or sent to a fiery pit of eternal suffering. Of course, these images do nothing to ease our fears regarding this transition from the earthly realm. It seems that we must succumb to endless speculation surrounding the *D-Word*, as neither religion, nor science, has found sufficient evidence to substantiate the whereabouts of our final resting place.

This eternal quandary could potentially be answered by the insights of what is commonly regarded as an ancient truth, and a modern mystery. The Near Death Experience (NDE) is often described as a mystical encounter, commonly experienced by someone whom doctors have reported as clinically dead before eventually, and often miraculously, being revived. The NDE gained widespread public attention during the mid '70s when Dr. Raymond Moody, a world-renowned scholar, published the book, *Life After Life*, presenting a thorough investigation into the subject. Yet Moody certainly wasn't the first to explore this subject. Plato's *Republic*, written in 360 BC, tells the story of a soldier named Er who had an NDE after being killed in battle. Similar accounts can be found throughout Greek, Egyptian and Roman literature. However it was the publication of Moody's book that sparked international interest, educating the masses through the sale of 13 million copies worldwide.

In response to reports in the 1991 National Gallup Poll that the number of Americans who had an NDE rose from eight million in the late '80s, to thirteen million in the early '90s, a group of independent researchers (including Moody) decided to form the International Association for Near-Death Studies (IANDS) for the purpose of further exploration. They began collecting thousands of individual NDE accounts in which survivors consistently recalled similar events: "They remembered a feeling of being detached from the physical body and an ability to float freely around the scene of their death. From this perspective, even though their heart had stopped beating and they were no longer breathing, they could clearly see relatives, or doctors, and nurses working to save their life. Some were even able to hear the unspoken thoughts of those around them and were surprisingly always able to confirm these after their recovery." The most interesting aspect of this research came from the subjects who temporarily reached the other side. Rather than confrontations with a white-bearded man, the majority found themselves: "Immersed in an all-encompassing and overwhelming feeling of love, unlike anything they'd ever experienced before." They often said that, "This was the most calm and peaceful thing that had ever happened," leaving them with the comfort and certainty that the afterlife is nothing to be scared of. Interestingly, Dr. Melvin Morse, an American pediatrician and neuroscientist who set out to disprove the validity of NDE's during the '80s, found that the hundreds of children he interviewed actually shared identical experiences. One of them, an eight-year-old named Chris, was resuscitated when his heart stopped beating because of kidney failure. Afterwards, he told Dr. Morse, "I have a wonderful secret to tell you. I was climbing a staircase to heaven." Morse's subjects reported the same thing over and over again, claiming that: "The end-of-life is serene and joyful, a welcome event not to be feared." Morse, a leading figure in the field of NDE research, is the author of numerous books including *Closer to the Light*.

The founders of IANDS concluded that the extensive research they collected provides incontrovertible evidence of NDE's, demonstrating that: "These are non-discriminatory, encountered by people from all walks of life with the overwhelming majority normal, level-headed individuals, thus ruling out the possibility that these are simply the fabrication of events by the fantasy-prone." This has surprised both doctors and academics, leading to the publication of numerous articles, in such prestigious medical journals as the *Lancet*, the *British Medical Journal*, the *Journal of Nervous and Mental Disease*, and the *American Journal of Psychiatry*, each discussing the existence of NDE's. Now, you may well have read articles that dismiss NDE's as "b*ll!sh*t", or you may hold a personal opinion about the feasibility of Near Death Experiences. Just for a moment, I'd like you to suspend any disbelief and consider the fact that many of our beliefs regarding the afterlife induce a certain level of fear, which feeds our denial of the *D-Word*. This can be a problem, especially if you intend to start creating *Your Legacy of Love* so you can take care of your loved ones. If, however, we pay heed to the observations of those who've experienced NDE's, then the picture of the afterlife seems much more appealing. They suggest that the terrifying train of the *D-Word* is really heading to destination Comfort Zone—a peaceful place where we are joyfully reunited with loved ones, and quickly relieved of all our earthly pains. Wouldn't it be easier to prepare for our departure and be more accepting of the *D-Word* if this really were the case? Should you want to explore the subject of NDE's a little more, there are many articles, books and organizations from which you can obtain more information and further explanation. I've listed a few in the Recommended Reading section at the back of this book, and you will find many more on the website: *www.realizethegift.com*

Accepting the Inevitable Sets You Free

Learning to accept the *D-Word* will have a powerful impact on your life. When you accept the inevitable, your life can change instantly. You can be relieved and liberated from all that constrains you. Our fear of the *D-Word* keeps us stuck in a state of apathy, unfulfilled, unfocused and off-purpose, accepting the things we don't like—work that is unsatisfying, situations that are demoralizing, or relationships that are unloving—as we tell ourselves that tomorrow we will find a way to fulfill our dreams.

If, however, you are someone who believes that tomorrow doesn't come, then you will live your life fully today, finding ways to fulfill your inner calling and desires. You will have a belief that you *are* capable of changing your life, and following your dreams. When you are living in denial of the *D-Word*, it's all too easy to take a temporary break from fully participating in this thing called life. Instead of investing your energy into things that align you with your truth, your time and attention is taken up with excuses, giving your clever little mind license to come up with countless reasons that keep your real desires and dreams suppressed. You become an expert in justification, kidding yourself with endless explanations, like "I'll do it later" or "I have to wait until I have more time / money / help or the kids have left home." You question the validity of your desires: "How can I make a difference?", "What will everyone think if I do that?" You question what you

deserve "Why should I have a better job / home / vacation / relationship than anyone else?", "It's not quite what I want, but I'll
take this for now, it won't be for long" . . . you know how it goes.
The mind enjoys this game. Repeatedly broadcasting unfounded
claims to convince our poor aching hearts that we can't achieve
our dreams, either because we are not good enough, intelligent,
attractive, strong, educated or brave enough to have the life, relationships or experiences that will fulfill our deepest desires.
Eventually we come to believe these misconceptions, swayed into
thinking that it's better to avoid making the changes necessary
to live our own individual truth. We find ways to maintain the
façade, with false smiles and retorts of "No, really, it's fine," as
yet another dream eludes us, as we passively allow those precious
seconds to tick by.

Hiding under this umbrella of denial temporarily allows you to
keep dry. You think it's pretty clever to stay out of the rain. Yet
as you bustle along, balancing this protective device above your
head, you may begin to notice the cumbersome and unwieldy
nature of this apparatus. You realize the effort required to hold
it upwards—to avoid poking someone's eye out—as you begin
to see how this umbrella has blocked your vision, casting a dark
shadow over your unique light. Looking back down Opportunity
Street, you see what you missed and wish you'd ventured out in
the rain. It's such a terrible shame—if only you'd played fully in
the game.

Others have been lucky enough to encounter life's unexpected storms, tornadoes or hurricanes, conditions that have forced the umbrella of denial from their tenacious grip, leaving them exposed and vulnerable—caught in the rain without any protection. Initially they cussed and complained, with shoulders hunched-up around their ears in an attempt to avoid the unwelcome invasion. They ran between doorways or held a bag above their heads, anything to stay in that dry and comfy place. But then something changed. They looked around, noticing the frustration and despair marked on the faces of those cramped under their umbrellas. It made them realize how stuck they'd been, so attached to staying comfortable and avoiding all the risks. In a flash, their attitude changed. They bravely stepped out into the rain and quickly began to enjoy the water splashing down their cheeks, laughing as it slowly trickled into their ears.

When was the last time you felt brave enough to play in the rain? You were probably a child when you last allowed a large droplet of water to form on the end of your nose and then drip off onto your shoe, as you tried to catch the next one with your tongue, smiling at the fun of it all! Oblivious to the concerned glances of the umbrella-laden passers by, you knew this was a game—to see how wet you could really get. Splashing in the puddles, you strode along, open and free, full of fun, ready to take on the world, fully aware that *this* is it, *now* is the only moment you have to live. Few of us live this way anymore because we believe there will always be another day to play. This belief is one that has gained strength in parallel with the continual increase of life expectancy. Because of healthier lifestyle choices and better medical care, genetics specialists such as Dr. Aubrey de Grey, Ph.D., of Cambridge College, prophesy that: "Within twenty-five years there is a 50 percent chance we will be able to live forever." With predictions like this, it's no wonder we choose not to think about "it" if we believe that it won't happen for another thirty, forty or fifty years, and if science has its way, never at all! But, when you realize that there were over fifty-six million deaths worldwide in 2007 (according to the World Health Organization)—that's nearly the same number of people that live in California! This means that thousands of parents, sisters, brothers and lovers, people just like you and me, are departing each and every day, year after year (even with the progress of modern medicine, high-tech innovations and anti-aging creams galore!).

Whether we're prepared to accept this or not, "it" will eventually happen to us all. Still, you might be thinking, "Why bother preparing now? Most people die from cancer, or heart disease and I won't get something like that until I'm really, really old." A fair observation, as non-communicable diseases (NCD's) are the common cause of death in the developed world. Sadly, these conditions can, and do, develop in people of all ages and walks of life, but they aren't the only thing that could happen to you. Unfortunately that old saying—you could get hit by a bus tomorrow—rings true; you just never know when the *D-Word* will come knocking at your door. You might assume you're safe while snuggled up in your PJ's at night, yet according to Nationmaster's central research database, 1,616 people die by simply falling out of their beds each year. And beware the next time you go out for a few beers, accidental alcohol poisoning finishes off a further 4,115 people annually. Even if you're a teetotaler, don't assume you are safe; the common cold, or Acute Nasopharyngitis—to use the correct medical term—wipes out 727 of the world's Kleenex users every year!

It's Your Choice: Hide or Realize the Gift!

If you still think you're invincible, take a moment to consider the potential for accidents in the home, at work, or while traveling around in cars, trains, planes, motorbikes and boats. Of course, if you happen to work in a high-risk field, such as the military, emergency services, security services, foreign aid or journalism, extreme sports, (highly stressed businessmen included!) or you are a professional explorer, sailor, pilot, astronaut or diver, then your chances of becoming a sudden fatality are much, much higher. No matter what your profession, you can't ignore the fact that the "what if" will eventually happen. Attempting to do so is ultimately senseless and could even be considered quite selfish. By ignoring "it" and failing to prepare, you pass up the chance to share your *Emotional Assets* with your survivors. Irrespective of whether you have two months or twenty years to live, each of us has a choice. To hide in denial of the *D-Word*, or take action, to discover what this experience involves for us and our loved ones, so we can do something about it now, before it's too late!

So, let's ditch the umbrella of denial and take some time to explore the *D-Word*—you'll be surprised to learn there is something to sweeten this bitter pill. Because, believe it or not, there's a silver lining, as those who've had an unexpected taste of their mortality have discovered, time after time. Tour de France champion Lance Armstrong maintains that cancer was the best thing that ever happened to him, despite leaving him physically and emotionally scarred. He explains that this life-threatening experience broadened his vision, helping him focus on the things that really mattered. His illness inspired him to contribute to the world at large, giving him the courage and motivation to start the Lance Armstrong Foundation. The foundation provides advice, education, advocacy, research and tools to help others in their battle against cancer, and is now recognized as one of the most influential organizations of its kind. Since his diagnosis Lance has added six more Tour de France titles to his many achievements and discovered material and emotional success beyond his wildest dreams.

Lance is by no means alone; many have been forced into the profound realization that "you only get one chance." After experiencing a disaster, disease, or tragic brush with the *D-Word*, they found their fears were forced into submission, and their desire to live an authentic life was ignited. Fully aware that we live today, but could die unannounced tomorrow, they found the courage to overcome the social, parental, religious, or self-imposed conditions that once prevented them from pursuing their dreams. Recognizing this truth transformed their lives; propelled into action, fueled with passion and purpose, they sought a more satisfying path. They gave up their justifications and excuses, with no more "I don't . . ." They found the courage to take whatever risks were required, to walk the most natural and rewarding path; to *give* love, *be* love, and *do* what they loved—while they still had the chance.

The Silver Lining: Start Following Your Bliss

Like Lance, many have set out to achieve the seemingly impossible, while others chose simply to re-focus on living and loving more fully. Take Duncan Ridgley, a British photographer who was traveling the world with his wife and three children, when a stopover in Arugam Bay, Sri Lanka resulted in disaster. They were woken by the roaring sound of water, and in just a few seconds the entire family was torn apart by the towering waves and ferocious currents of the 2004 Asian Tsunami. Duncan's twelve-year-old daughter was smashed against trees, cars, and buildings before managing to grab hold of a floating refrigerator. She clung on for dear life. The tendons in her foot had been ripped open by nails protruding from the debris, leaving a seriously painful gaping wound. Alone and petrified, she feared both for her parents' lives and her own. Miraculously, the entire Ridgley family survived and was eventually reunited.

Despite the ongoing flashbacks and strain of survivor's guilt, Duncan has a positive attitude about the after-effects of this terrifying ordeal. "Few things reinforce your compulsion to live for the moment than seeing your children seconds from possible death. So many people are working for an imaginary future time in their life, but we are in our lives now, this is it." This wake-up call convinced the Ridgleys to accept the inevitable and start taking some risks. They decided to continue their travels indefinitely, spending more time together as a family, and rather than return to the drudgery of a nine-to-five commuter life, they opened a web-based travel business. Duncan is thankful that they got a second chance, "I wake up in the morning and think, 'God, we might not have been able to do this,' life is so precious."

Without this sudden scrape with the *D-Word,* the Ridgelys may have returned to their routine existence, and continued the fear-induced façade to which so many of us succumb. Why is it that we remain stuck in this safe yet horribly unsatisfying place? Joseph Jaworski, one of the critically acclaimed authors of *Presence: Human Purpose and the Field of the Future,* believes it is our fear of living that holds us back. He writes, "I discovered that people are not really afraid of dying, they're afraid of not ever having lived, not ever having deeply considered their life's higher purpose, and not ever having stepped into that purpose and at least tried to make a difference in this world."

American philosopher Joseph Campbell notes that, "People say that what we're all seeking is the meaning of life. I don't think that's what we're seeking. I think what we're seeking is an experience of being alive, so that our life experiences on the purely physical plane will have resonance with our own innermost being and reality. What we actually feel is the rapture of being alive." Personally, I think the American actor Michael Landon (*Highway to Heaven*) expressed it best during an interview he gave with *Life* magazine when fighting pancreatic cancer: "Somebody should tell us right at the start of our lives that we are dying. Then, we might live life to the limit! Every minute of every day! DO IT, I SAY! WHATEVER IT IS YOU WANT TO DO! Do it NOW! There are only so many tomorrows . . ." Now, before you grab the book *1,000 Places to See Before You Die* and whisk your family off to every destination, take a moment to see how simple it can be to release your fears of death so you can start living your life more fully. You can start by asking the question "Is this right for me?" Applying it to all areas of your life—your relationships, career and lifestyle—then, when the heartfelt answer is "No," do something about it. Don't wait. Just make a change. Right then and there.

If it helps, imagine you only have three or six months to live, stop and take the time to listen to the needs of your heart, noticing what dreams and desires bubble to the surface. They might be hard to hear or feel at first, but persevere. This practice can take months to master if you've been ignoring these messages for some time. Keep meditating on this question until the ideas that tug at your heart get louder and stronger. Sit in silence, go to a quiet place or just get away from the people who keep telling you that you can't have whatever it is you want. That is their belief. It doesn't have to be yours. It will, of course, take time to change your mind and form a true belief that you can and will have what you desire, just remember that the *D-Word* is always lurking around the corner— it's all the motivation you'll ever require. Eventually, as you learn to listen to these inner desires, you will find the courage to act. As time goes on, your passion will overrun the fears that get formed within your head and you'll find it so much easier to follow your heart.

You'll find this practice will quickly dissolve any murky areas in your life, leaving you free to live your future: to choose a vibrant and fulfilling life, to learn what and who it is you love. Then you'll be able to "follow your bliss" so that when you finally reach those Great Pearly Gates there will be no question of looking back over your shoulder with any regret. Instead, you'll be content in knowing that you lived your life fully. With a satisfied smile, and your head held high, you'll float right on in.

PART II

✻✻✻✻✻✻✻✻✻✻✻✻✻✻✻✻✻✻✻✻✻✻✻✻✻✻

The Gift

✻✻✻✻✻✻✻✻✻✻✻✻✻✻✻✻✻✻✻✻✻✻✻✻✻✻

5

Good Guidance

Advice is like snow. The softer it falls, the longer it dwells,
and the deeper it sinks into the mind
— Samuel Taylor-Coleridge, Poet

Helen Harcombe was just like any other mother, focused on giving her seven-year-old daughter Ffion the best in parental care to ensure a healthy and happy upbringing. But when Helen was tragically diagnosed with terminal breast cancer at twenty-eight, and Ffion, upon learning of her mother's illness, had asked, "How will you look after me, Mommy?" Helen had replied, "Don't worry. I'm going to heaven and I will look after you from there."

Helen wanted to know that her parenting principles would extend well beyond her lifetime, and so, true to her word, Helen secretly penned an instructional "How-to" guide, detailing the things that her husband Anthony could do to bring up their daughter Ffion in her absence. This included suggestions to: "Check hair for nits regularly. Bath and hair wash every other night, at least. No child of mine is to be smelly;" ideas for Christmas stocking fillers,

"Chocolates, hair bobbles, make-up, fun stuff, etc." and practical advice on household matters: "Bedding should be changed once a fortnight, more if sweaty." Helen even issued a gentle warning, "Keep in touch with Fi's godparents and my friends, especially Mom and Dad or . . . I'll be back to haunt you!"

The Power of Parenting by Proxy

Helen's "Mommy Manual" made news headlines around the world as psychologists and family support groups hailed the therapeutic benefits of Helen's approach to parenting by proxy. Jill Templeman, a family support leader for Marie Curie Cancer Care, applauded the positive effect this ongoing legacy would have for Helen's surviving family, "This is a lovely and invaluable thing for Anthony and Ffion, it's left them with a continual bond. It must have been very therapeutic for Helen." Anthony was especially grateful for such *Good Guidance*, at a time when he had to adapt to the role of stand-in mother, while also coming to terms with the loss of his wife. Helen had understood that she couldn't necessarily rely on fate, or her beloved husband to take care of her surviving daughter, so she wrote this manual to ensure she could continue parenting Ffion from beyond the grave. Because Helen had been the primary caregiver in Ffion's life, she was understandably concerned that her husband was not as confident with the all-important aspects of the school routine, or the finer elements of mothering a young girl. Anthony was handed the three-page guide by Helen's parents shortly after she died. Commenting in an article for the *Times* newspaper, Anthony said, "When it comes to Ffion I'm always thinking, 'How would Helen have done this?' The advice she left has definitely helped me be a better parent."

Millions of children, young and old, tragically lose one or both parents, leaving them to live without their Mom or Dad. Of the 56 million deaths that occur annually, the World Health Organization reports that each one has a major impact on at least four family members. That means over 200 million people must learn to cope with the challenges of loss each year. These survivors—adults and children alike—will be in need of guidance. Something like a "Mommy Manual" to help them adjust to the change in their circumstances, some advice on the practical issues they face, as well as ongoing support to help them come to terms with and recover from their grief.

Helen Harcombe's "Mommy Manual"

❃ Make sure to serve food with veg/peas – get fruit down her. Don't let her live off cans, noodles and toast, etc.

❃ Buy a new school uniform every September (cardigan, trousers, skirt, dress, and short-sleeve shirts – you might be able to use the previous year's if tidy enough). If not, chuck out—no daughter of mine is to look scruffy!

❃ Dress her trendily out of school – boot-cut jeans, trendy boots. Go to tidy shops!

❃ Regular trims on hair. Ensure hair is tied back for school in a neat parting, no bump. Smooth with comb if necessary.

❃ Go to parents' evenings—all of them. Homework. Keep an eye out for bullying or problems in school. Check schoolbag every night for spelling, letters, etc.

❃ Before long, put a lock on bathroom door. She will appreciate this as she gets older.

❃ Don't just take down my photos. Keep them safe for Ffion and send flowers to me, at least on Mother's day, my B-day, Fi's B-day, our anniversary, but in-between would be nice!

It will take time for your loved ones to adapt to life after losing you—the person who is central to their existence—their parent, partner, life-long companion, or lover, the person who guided them, supported them, cooked for them, bought presents, paid the bills, planned vacations, and organized family gatherings. There are probably times when they didn't realize just how important you were, but once you're gone, they'll appreciate what a miracle-worker you were. They will become aware of the true extent of what you did for them, even the small seemingly insignificant things, like how you knew who to call when the washing machine broke down or what brand of cookies to buy.

If you think back to the last time you stayed away from home for a week or two, you'll probably remember that you got more than one call from your husband, partner or friend asking "Where do I find . . . ?", "How do I . . . ?" or "What do I do with...?" Perhaps a crisis occurred and the calls were of a more serious nature, with the enquirer asking, "Are they allergic to...?" or "What medication should I . . . ?" or "Where do I find the gas. . . ?" Now magnify these calls for help by a few thousand, and you'll soon get an idea of the need your loved ones will have for your ongoing guidance once you've passed on.

Who'll Support Them?

Who is going to know these things once you've gone? Who'll take care of fixing things, managing the money and paying the bills? Who will remember all the things your children favored? Who is going to maintain relations with family and friends? Who will support them? The absence of your ways and wisdom will leave a big gap in the lives of your survivors, especially for those who are dependant on you:

❋   Children, teenagers, young adults and grandchildren.

❋   Elderly relatives, especially parents and spouses.

❋   Partners or ex-spouses who remain as single parents.

❋   Long-term friends and caregivers.

❋   Anyone who has experienced a prior loss.

❋   People suffering from addictions or low self-esteem.

❋   People with mental illness or depression.

❋   Anyone lacking the support of family and friends.

Everyone has different needs and some will require a greater degree of support and guidance after you are gone. The advice you would leave for a seven-year-old won't be suitable for your adult daughter, elderly spouse or a partner, who must now learn to support the remaining family as a single parent. The needs of each person will depend on their age, health, emotional stability and their dependency on you—an important factor to consider when creating Your Legacy of Love. Typically, there will be one or two people who will be severely affected by the loss because they're so dependant on you. It's usually pretty easy to identify them. Bear in mind that elderly partners, young children and those with special needs are likely to feel more abandoned than other family members who have people they can turn to. Don't assume that people will cope just because they seem old enough.

My brother and I were young adults when Mom died, so other people assumed we'd be okay. They didn't take into account the fact that Mom and Dad divorced when we were very young. As a single-parent family we had become totally reliant on Mom as our primary caregiver. Dad was re-married and had two other children, so his hands were pretty full, and even though he lived close by, he wasn't able to play much of a role in our lives. While we were very close to Francis, Mom's partner of ten years, he had his own apartment, which meant that after she died, technically we were on our own. Having inherited the family home, Jacob and I were faced with many challenging decisions:

I'm really not sure what to do about the house. The garden you invested so much time in has already grown wild! It seems crazy to leave it empty and not rent it out. I just can't imagine having anyone else living there; it would be horrible. The other option is to sell. But that seems so final. I don't think we're ready for that yet, and I have no idea where we would go during the holidays. I'd hate not being able to go "home".

We could definitely have benefited from the guidance of someone more experienced than we were. However, this was only the beginning. In the months and years ahead, many more challenges presented themselves—practical issues, emotional and relationship problems, questions and queries about life, faith and love. We were learning to cope with the day-to-day issues of running a home and a family, while struggling to come to terms with our loss. There was so much we needed to learn and we required a lot more help than we cared to admit.

You Could Use a Trustworthy Captain

Your survivors will need a lot more than a "little black book" of phone numbers for maintenance guys, or ideas on how to save money on the heating bills. Reminders and tips on practical issues will definitely be helpful (especially if you've been the one primarily responsible for such things), but what your loved ones really need is advice on all the issues that will continue to affect them. Give some thought to the following subjects and how you can start "parenting by proxy" by offering *Good Guidance* to your surviving family:

✻　　　Health, nutrition and general well-being.

✻　　　Education, personal development and career.

✻　　　Finances, investments and money-management.

✻　　　Management and maintenance of the home.

✻　　　Friends, relationships, pets and family.

✻　　　Religion, traditions and spirituality.

✻　　　Bereavement and grief support.

You could start with a simple list of Top Tips, or, like Helen Harcombe, you could write a detailed How-to guide. Maybe even put together a recommended reading list of books that will help with specific subjects that your survivors will struggle with in your absence. If you have the skills and equipment, you could also capture and pass on your wisdom through a video or Webisode, leaving them the gift of an instructional film or DVD—just like Bob did in the film *My Life*. Just make sure you choose your topics carefully. Some subjects won't necessarily appeal, and you don't want everyone to remember you as a real bore!

It's important that you're conscious of the impact your *Good Guidance* will have on your survivors, as anything you leave will inevitably be perceived as your dying wish, and the potency of your words will be significantly amplified. Your imparted wisdom has the potential to be very damaging, especially if your message is not a loving one. If, for example, you place unrealistic demands on them, or request that they live in accordance with your rules, you will limit their opportunity to learn for themselves and will not be honoring their individuality. The end result could be a lifetime of guilt, anger and lack of fulfillment. Remember, your legacy is about love, not an exercise in control or emotional blackmail!

The *Good Guidance* you are going to leave will help your loved ones in many ways, but it will only go so far. When grief takes over, life changes so dramatically that it's impossible to forecast all of your loved ones' needs. There is, however, one thing you can predict: that they will be in need of grief support. That's why it's a good idea to find a captain to man your ship. Someone who can mentor them—offering real-time guidance—perhaps a professional advisor, a trustworthy friend or a family member who can be relied upon to give love and support. If you have young children, you may already have chosen godparents for this purpose. However, if it's not traditional in your faith to select someone to act in *loco parentis* then you'll want to consider the idea of recruiting someone to fulfill this role. Imagine you are looking for a trustworthy captain to man your ship—someone who can support and steer your survivors through the bumpy seas of bereavement. This person will be responsible for the ongoing care and welfare of your dependants, navigating them through the journey of grief.

As with any effective recruiting process, you'll need to establish the exact role, the skills required to do the job and the terms of agreement before you start looking for a mentor. Ideally, you want someone who has both practical abilities and a compassionate approach to the needs of your loved ones—it will certainly help if they've been through a loss before, otherwise they'll have a hard time understanding the challenges your survivors will face. When you've identified someone who meets your criteria, you should make sure they understand all the responsibilities they will be undertaking, and let them into the secret of your family's favorite brand of cookies!

Many people don't really understand how to treat someone who has experienced a loss, and they don't appreciate the extent of change or the breadth of challenges that survivors experience. As a result, the common response is to ignore or avoid the bereaved. This can be a painful blow for survivors, as friends, other family members and familiar support networks start to disappear— another reason for having a mentor, someone who can be a loyal and stable support during this time of sudden change.

When someone dies, it can cause a dramatic shift in the view of the world for the bereaved, affecting attitudes and interests in all areas of life: relationships, faith, ability to perform, leisure interests, finances, health and home. Activities that previously seemed fun or exciting—sports, leisure activities and socializing—can, in light of the loss, become quite unappealing. Unfortunately, as the bereaved retreat from their normal activities, they will find themselves separated from friends or family members with whom they previously shared such interests. This can add insult to injury, increasing the sense of isolation and their feelings of loss, something I quickly learned:

> The girls went out this evening, but I wasn't invited. I guess they assumed I wouldn't want to go. They were right. The idea of dancing in a noisy club just doesn't appeal to me anymore. Still it hurts, not to be invited.

Just as you think you're acclimatizing to the departure of one person, you find you're facing a mass exodus. When Mom died, at least four of my supposed friends literally dropped me and disappeared overnight. So much for loyalty! Your survivors will all react in different ways to their loss. Some will become extremely protective of remaining family members for fear that something will happen to them too. Normal everyday tasks, such as driving, walking to the shops, playing a sport, or taking the train to work take on a whole new meaning. My attitude towards my brother's surfing activities changed considerably after Mom died:

> Jacob called this afternoon. It's funny, we fought so much before, but now we get on brilliantly. But I do wish he wouldn't go surfing, it scares me now. I couldn't bear to lose him too—it would kill me!

Certain types of loss will accentuate this reaction—especially if the death was accidental or very sudden. The resulting fear factor, if left unchecked, can get in the way of healthy recovery, causing survivors to become unnecessarily controlling and nagging, or timid and withdrawn. These are the kind of symptoms and effects of grief that your chosen mentor should be aware of. If, however, you don't know anyone with this kind of experience, you can direct your loved ones to one of the many bereavement support groups, such as The Dougy Center, Compassionate Friends or The Grief Recovery Institute whose book, The *Grief Recovery Handbook: The Action Program for Moving Beyond Death, Divorce and Other Losses* would be an excellent gift to leave your survivors. You can also find a list of international bereavement support organizations at: *www.realizethegift.com*

To Encourage Their Healthy Recovery

In the immediate aftermath of their loss, your survivors may be too overwhelmed or shocked to receive the *Good Guidance* you've left behind, but as life gets back to some sense of normality, they'll slowly come to appreciate the immense value of your gift. The need for help on practical issues commonly lasts no more than twelve to eighteen months, although experts typically claim that the grieving process lasts somewhere between one to eight years. However, grief is an extremely individual experience; what takes one person a month may take another three to five years. The degree and duration of grief will depend on the nature of relationship with the person who died, the quality of that relationship, the time they had to prepare for the loss, their personality, and whether or not they had experienced prior losses. Needless to say, your survivors will probably benefit from your *Good Guidance* and the help of your designated mentor for quite some time, because the emotional, behavioral and mental issues often continue to present challenges for many years. Unfortunately, many of those who've dealt with a loss assume that the bereaved should recover in accordance with what worked in their own experience. To prevent your loved ones from being subjected to such conditioning or having the *Must Move On* mantra forced on them, you will want to offer them advice on what is considered to be a healthy recovery.

The path through grief can be gentle for your survivors, if they are fully supported and encouraged to express their emotions, so they can progress naturally towards a healthy recovery. Through my work counseling survivors, I have been able to establish a Model of Response to Grief, which shows the typical emotional responses that the bereaved experience during three phases—*Reaction*, *Reflection* and *Recovery*—as they learn to fully assimilate the loss into their life, and reach a place of peace. This model gives you some idea of the time it can take for the bereaved to begin their recovery and shows you the breadth and duration of the emotional impact on your survivors' lives.

The Three R's: Model of Response to Grief

REACTION	REFLECTION	RECOVERY
1 – 2 Years	1 – 4 Years	2 – 10 Years
Guilt	Release	Hopeful
Shock	Isolated	Accepting
Disbelief	Directionless	Focused
Heartbreak	Jealous	Motivated
Blame	Exhausted	Settled
Numbness	Worried	Whole
Apathy	Resentful	Energetic
Frightened	Depressed	Compassionate
Confused	Angry	Empathetic
Alone	Stressed	Normal
Relief	Incomplete	Philosophical
Destroyed	Restless	Peace

After your death, your bereaved must first face the *Reaction* period, which is a very difficult time as they have to face life for the first time without your love and support. Emotions are running high during this phase and the issues facing your survivors will include practical, spiritual, emotional and physical reactions to the loss. This might include a very real sense of heartbreak, as if something is stabbing or twisting in the chest area. Numbness, shock and total disbelief are common reactions to death. Depending on how the loss has occurred, some people may shift quickly from the *Reaction* to the *Reflection* phase, especially if the death has been expected for some time, or the person who has passed is elderly and has led a full life.

During the *Reflection* period, the bereaved will begin to assimilate the loss, meaning that they will develop the ability to rely on themselves as they become accustomed to their independence, and learn to be open to new experiences and relationships once again. During this phase, a lot of readjustment takes place. Philosophical and spiritual concerns will arise as they begin to find answers to the question of "Why?" and learn to deal with the reality that death is ever-present in our lives.

Over time, the negative responses to this loss begin to fade, and more positive emotions frequently arise. This helps improve their outlook on life, moving them into the more hopeful *Recovery* stage. When a positive state of mind predominates, survivors typically find that the loss has been accepted on an emotional, spiritual and physical level, leaving them free to live without the burden of grief. Often, the bereaved will experience these emotional responses at random, bouncing between these states, even when they appear to have progressed from one phase to the next. This is perfectly normal, although the frequency of these fluctuations will vary from person to person. Many will suffer mood swings, depression, insomnia and extreme fatigue as a result of this emotional roller-coaster ride. This can severely affect their ability to perform professionally, and their potential to form and maintain healthy personal relationships until they have reached full recovery. During the *Reaction* phase, appetite is also commonly affected and in severe cases can develop into eating disorders, while other health problems, such as eczema, asthma and migraines may suddenly appear out of the blue or become exacerbated. These symptoms may sound dreadful, but they are common aspects of grief and will usually only last for a short time.

There are, however, certain signs that a mentor, or your remaining family, should be aware of—warnings that suggest the bereaved may have entered the *Danger Zone* due to unresolved or abnormal grief. These signs include suddenly withdrawing from society for extended periods, ignoring family members, or refusing to talk about the deceased. Ongoing depression is another obvious symptom and can manifest in the loss of a sense of self or debilitating emotional pain, which can impair the ability to function healthily in work, relationships and life. Unexpressed anger, repressed emotions and denial of the death are commonly the cause of this. Abnormal grief can create paranoia about one's own or another's health. For example, someone who has lost a loved one to cancer may become convinced that they, too, have the disease.

In the extreme, abnormal or unresolved grief may lead to suicidal thoughts, eating disorders or excessive substance abuse. Other signs of the *Danger Zone* include:

❋   Thinking or planning to commit suicide.

❋   Detachment from life or activities they used to enjoy.

❋   Excessive or unusual level of drinking or drug taking.

❋   Bruises or cuts on limbs possibly caused by self-harm.

❋   Irregular eating patterns or odd behaviors around food.

❋   Self-imposed isolation for an unusually long time.

❋   Irregular spending or a sudden accumulation of stuff.

❋   Obsessive behavior over cleanliness and health.

❋   Refusal to talk about the loss or obsession about it.

These are things you could discuss with family members in advance so they are aware, not only of what to expect, but also to know what is healthy and what is not. Your mentor or remaining family should also seek professional assistance if they see any of these symptoms in your survivors. If left unchecked, these symptoms can result in thinking and behaviors that can develop into serious mental health issues. However, such consequences are unlikely for your survivors because you will have equipped them with all the tools for a healthy recovery, leaving them your *Good Guidance* and the loving support of a capable mentor and trustworthy captain to man the ship in your absence.

6

Future Surprises

As for the future, your task is not to foresee it, but
to enable it — Antoine de Saint Exupery, Author

The future is a destination for realizing hopes and dreams. Normally it is a place where there is something to look forward to, perhaps an organized event or forthcoming festivity, a special birthday party, a wedding or an annual celebration, like Christmas. These joyful days are preceded by a sense of expectation and excitement, filled with fun and laughter, and shared with the people we love. Often these mark rites of passage or important life transitions, uniting family and friends in celebrations, which create treasured memories that brighten our lives.

Yet for the bereaved, these festive times can take on a whole new meaning. They can easily become the cause for suffering, rather than days of joy and celebration. The cards, presents, gifts and phone calls received by others often serve as a painful reminder that they won't be getting any such thing from the person who has gone. These celebrations are no longer something to get excited about as these days emphasize the absence of a loved one, bring-ing back painful memories and magnifying the sense of separa-tion—instead they become *Lonely Landmarks*.

Lonely Landmarks: 2, 4, 10 Years From Now

Christmas was the first official celebration after Mom died. It was seven weeks after her funeral, and I was still very raw. The pros-pect of Christmas at home without her was dismal so I was ex-tremely grateful when my aunt and uncle invited us to stay. In the preceding weeks, I had kept busy buying presents, which distract-ed me from the uncomfortable feelings brewing just beneath the surface. I was dreading the forthcoming day, as I knew it would be awful. When I woke on Christmas morning, my first thought was "Don't think about her," but I couldn't help it. Moments lat-er the tears were trickling down my face. I wanted to scream, "What's the point? It's never going to be the same without her," but I didn't want to upset everyone. I looked down at the empty space on my bed. Normally, Momma Santa would have placed a stocking there, but not this year. The silly red sock embroidered with my name and stuffed with inexpensive and humorous items had been a traditional feature on Christmas day every year since I was born. To me, this tradition symbolized my mother's love, an expression of her time, care and attention, which demonstrated her understanding of me. The empty space at the foot of my bed was a stark reminder that Mom was gone. That from now on, no one was going to fulfill this caring role in my life. The rest of the day passed by in a swollen-eyed blur. Christmas never would be the same again. Although the following year wasn't quite so bad, other special occasions re-ignited my terrible sense of loss. Even after two or three years had passed, when I seemed to have begun recovering from my grief, one of these *Lonely Landmarks* would come along and take me right back to square one. Yet, other people just didn't seem to appreciate the difficulty of those days.

For the first few months after Mom died, everyone had rallied around, offering condolences and support. Recognizing that I was on an emotional roller-coaster ride, they acknowledged the fact that I was going through a major readjustment. But two years later, when my graduation day came about, it seemed that no one understood the difficulties. Everyone's parents were there that day and time after time, someone would say, "Oh, are your Mom and Dad here?" I did my best to respond pleasantly.

It is quite typical for the bereaved to receive great support initially—offers to cook food, help with travel and transportation, assistance with funeral arrangements or financial aid—but this rarely continues beyond the first twelve months. Fast-forward two, four or ten years and the support, gentle words and understanding have usually disappeared. However, your survivors' need for support will continue for many years to come, as the celebrations: annual holidays, birthdays, weddings, graduations, births and Christmases don't stop coming, and with them, a continual reminder that *you* aren't there to share the special occasion. I found that the major events, which marked turning points in my life, all became *Lonely Landmarks*: The day that I graduated from college, my thirtieth birthday, every year on Mother's day, and May 10 (Mom's birthday). I was bombarded with the negative emotions of grief, even though years had passed since Mom's death. Sadly, I know it doesn't end there. There are more *Lonely Landmarks* on the horizon, days when Mom's spirited presence will be sorely missed, and I will struggle with the fact that she isn't on the guest list for the day of my wedding or the birth of my first child. I am sure that these future events will be incredibly hard, and no doubt, a box of tissues will be required!

When the "Firsts" Arrive

Each *Lonely Landmark* will, in time, be less of a reminder of the loss. As the years pass, the bereaved begin to adjust to their new life, building new relationships and forming fresh memories, which will help to make those special occasions easier to bear. Eventually, these events will be a cause for celebration again, and the bereaved will find they experience joy, excitement and laughter once more. Nevertheless, there will still be days when they experience a resurgence of grief. These are the "firsts," the days when the bereaved encounter a major transition or important event for the first time after a loss. You will often hear the bereaved place great emphasis on these "firsts":

"It's going to be my *first* birthday without Dad."

"This is our *first* Christmas without our son Paul."

"This is my *first* holiday as a single person."

"This is my *first* child without Mom to help me."

"This will be my *first* wedding without my husband."

It doesn't matter if this event comes one month, two years or ten years after the loss, by the very nature of it being the "first" time this event is happening without you, it's guaranteed to have a powerful and painful impact on your survivors. More often than not, these events will take place outside of the twelve-month time-frame that others consider an "acceptable" period for grief. Therefore, partygoers, friends, and even family members might be oblivious or unaware of how painful this can be. In an attempt to help, they may offer well intended advice, like:

"Come on, it's been months, you must be over it now?"

"Don't ruin the day for everyone else."

"You still have your son, make it special for him."

"It's your birthday, be happy!"

"Come out—you need cheering up!"

"They would want you to have fun."

"Please don't cry, you'll upset everyone."

Despite their good intention, such counsel is very misplaced and can hurt the feelings of survivors or make them feel that they've been totally misunderstood. Again, that's where your mentor can be a real savior—as someone who understands the impact of these "firsts," they can empathize with your survivors and help them to focus on the more positive aspects of the occasion, encouraging them to remember the joyous moments from previous celebrations.

However, this doesn't have to be the sole responsibility of your mentor. There are ways that you can support your survivors and help reduce their suffering during these "firsts." You can leave a special gift, something to help them remember how much you cared. This gift is a *Future Surprise*—something you buy, create or arrange in advance, so it can be delivered to your survivors in the future, at a time when your absence will really be felt.

Just imagine your children, many years from now, receiving little surprise reminders of you, a message of congratulations for their birthday captured in a letter, speech or video. Picture your wife or husband receiving a poem or a present, something that's been kept safe until a special anniversary, when it's personally delivered into their welcoming hands. Envision your daughter on her wedding day—see the smile on her face—as she's presented with your *Future Surprise*, a beautiful bouquet of flowers or a keepsake, together with your blessings for a happy marriage.

The following days are "firsts" when your loved ones will really cherish such a gift from you, but there may also be holidays specific to your faith or tradition, which, although not mentioned here, are clearly going to be a challenging time for your survivors:

❋ Exams, graduation and important tests.

❋ First day at school or job interviews.

❋ Mother's Day, Father's Day and Valentine's Day.

❋ Pregnancy or the birth of a child.

❋ Anniversaries, engagements and weddings.

❋ Special birthdays: 16, 18, 21, 30, 40 and 60.

❋ Christenings, confirmation and other rites of passage.

❋ Bar or Bat Mitzvah and coming of age ceremonies.

❋ Diwali, Ramadan, Passover, Yom Kippur and Hanukkah.

❋ Christmas, Easter and New Year's Eve.

With An Act of Courage

The question is "What do you leave?" for a *Future Surprise*. Well, really it all depends on how much time and energy you have to invest. If your remaining time is short, it will require a real act of courage to create your *Future Surprise*, as John Reiss—a man who was diagnosed with an inoperable brain tumor—discovered. John only had a couple of months, maybe even weeks left to live, so he decided to write his young son Felix some letters. In an article published by *The Guardian* newspaper, his surviving wife Madeleine describes the impact that John's *Future Surprise* had on her family:

"I think John wanted to be alone, but I couldn't have stayed anyway. Those last words were very private ones. He had to stretch this one afternoon into all the years he wouldn't have. He only managed to write three letters: for Felix's thirteenth birthday, his eighteenth and then, strangely, his nineteenth. I think Felix at twenty-one was just too far in the distance. John died quietly when Felix was almost four and the three blue envelopes lay in my desk for the next ten years. Every now and again I would take them out and look at them. Seeing John's handwriting always caused a shock, a small tremor of recognition. I would sometimes wonder if I should open them and check what was inside. I worried that since he had been so ill, so nuked with medication, they might be incoherent and scary. I was concerned that since Felix had so few memories of his father he would not be able to put these words into any sort of context. But the letters were not mine to read. On Felix's thirteenth birthday, I waited until there were just the two of us. Felix was tentative, a little scared. I had the feeling that by opening the envelope he was releasing his father's long-held breath. It was a lovely letter. It said all the things it needed to, that thirteen was a significant birthday, that he hoped Felix was happy and that he hoped he knew he had been loved. "It's as if he is talking to me," said Felix, and then we both cried for a while. Felix is now seventeen, and there will be delivery of the second letter soon. I don't know what's in it, but I am confident that John will have found the right words. It was the ultimate act of courage, braver than all the stoicism that had gone before, that he was able to imagine life continuing without him and to pass on his small time capsules of love."

These loving letters were a priceless gift for Felix, but it's clear they also benefited John by helping him to achieve some sense of peace with his own departure. Yet, one has to wonder what John might have done if he'd been blessed with more time. John probably wasn't motivated to prepare this *Future Surprise* any earlier because, like so many, he thought he had all the time in the world, or was scared, and wanted to put it off. The problem with delaying this activity is that sickness, medications and debilitating symptoms can make it impossible to create, or plan your *Future Surprise* at the very end. If you put this off in the belief that the worst will never happen to you, then, should your life suddenly be cut short, you run the risk of leaving your survivors empty-handed. Sadly, the children suffer most when this is the case, as they have a greater need for a continuing bond and reminders of the love that their parents had for them.

Donna Schuurman, Director of the Dougy Center for Grieving Children and Families in Portland, OR, comments: "For one boy, that meant saving his mother's voice on an answering machine for many years." She adds, "Children have an incredible desire to know who the deceased person was, otherwise they're left only with their memories." That's why it's important to give some thought to the *Future Surprise* you will leave behind. Even if you're the picture of perfect health, you could take an afternoon to write some simple love letters—just like John Reiss, or *Billy Elliot's* mom. Think of this as a little something "just in case," that's stored away to guarantee that your family, especially your children, will never miss out when those "firsts" come around.

While this might sound easy enough, you may have to overcome feelings of hopelessness at the idea that one day you won't be around to join in with these occasions. Do you remember when I said that it takes courage to create *Your Legacy of Love*? Well, that's exactly where your *Future Surprise* can help. By thinking about what you want to leave behind you have to focus on the needs of your survivors, rather than your own. Once you shift the focus from you to other people and begin concentrating on their future, rather than your own, you'll find that feelings of helplessness will begin to dissolve. The reward for relieving the suffering of others is a deeper peace of mind and a comfort in knowing that you have done something to make a difference. By creating a *Future Surprise*, you are not tempting fate or admitting defeat; what you are doing is brave, admirable, kind and caring, and something that will bring your loved ones more joy than you can imagine.

Most of the examples I've given for *Future Surprises* involve letters or simple messages, but you certainly don't have to stop there. With just a little vision and resourcefulness, you can develop surprises that will really bring a smile to your survivors' faces, by tailoring them to your loved ones' hobbies, desires, and needs. I often work with people, helping them to do this, and the ideas they come up with always surprise me. One woman, whom I'll call Rachel, wanted to leave something special for her sister, so she designed a *Future Surprise* around her sister's hobby of collecting charms. She bought ten little charms, each symbolic of a special time shared with her beloved sister, and tucked each one inside a birthday card. She left them in the safe hands of her lawyer, who agreed to deliver the cards to her sister Ann every year on her birthday.

When I spoke to Ann about her experience, she said, "I'm always so excited about receiving these little surprises. They bring back wonderful memories. It makes me feel like she's still here with me." These gifts were an important part of Ann's healing process, leaving her with a continuing bond that will always remind her of how much her sister cared.

You Can Create Something Special

Rachel's idea was perfect for her sister Ann, but a gift of charms won't do much for a teenage son! You'll have to give some thought to the needs, hobbies and interests of your loved ones if you want your *Future Surprise* to be adored. To give you some more ideas, I've included examples from other clients here. I'll begin with Roger, who was planning a *Future Surprise* for his six-year-old son. Roger was fifty-five when his son was born, and since poor heart health ran in his family, he was concerned about his future. He began planning well in advance for the "what if" even though he was in good health, because Roger knew there was a possibility that he could be gone by the time his son graduated.

Roger said, "I know that one day my son will go to college, but as an elderly parent, I may not be around to see him graduate, so I want to leave a *Future Surprise* that will help him to celebrate, with me by his side." Roger wanted his son to know that, whatever path his son chose, he would be able to succeed. "I want him to know that I'll be proud of him and love him no matter what he does. I'm in cahoots with my wife, she's much younger than me, so we expect she'll still be around to organize it all.

We've planned a big party to be held at his first school—where the foundations of his education were put in place—and we want to invite all his friends, teachers and mentors, everyone who will have played a part in getting him to that point in his life." Roger spent a lot of time thinking about this *Future Surprise* and preparing mini-surprises within the surprise. He explained, "We're going to have a band sing him my favorite song, 'We Are the Champions,' by Queen. Whenever I've struggled in life, I've put this on, and it's always lifted my spirits and helped me believe in myself. I want to share that with him."

Although Roger's *Future Surprise* might seem rather elaborate to some, just remember you don't have to follow any specific rules. Everyone's *Legacy of Love* will be unique, and you should only do what's right for you and your surviving loved ones. Roger's idea involved a lot of organization, and he was lucky to have a team he could rely on. You may not have this luxury, or there may be obstacles that hold you back from such lavish surprises, such as budgetary constraints, or a lack of time to organize. If these are a concern, you could borrow an idea or two from the lovely Louise—a married woman in her late thirties, who had no children but a rare illness that meant she would soon be leaving behind a much-loved husband. Louise had a powerful, yet simple, idea for her *Future Surprise*—a gift to her husband for their wedding anniversary. Louise said, "I want him to have something by which he can remember me. I'd like to give him an oak sapling. Something he can plant, a symbol of hope that will slowly grow in strength. I think that by watching the tree grow, it will help him appreciate the patience he'll need to overcome the loss of me in his life. In springtime, when the shoots come through, it will remind him that there's always regeneration, something new to look forward to."

Katie had a similar idea. She was also leaving a long-term partner and wanted her to know that she would always love her. She planned a surprise holiday and was relying on her brother to organize the trip, using the fund she'd set up with money saved from her salary every month. She hoped her partner would take the trip the year after she'd passed, ideally on her birthday. Katie left specific instructions that she was to take someone with her, because she didn't want her feeling lonely. The *Future Surprise* was a weeklong trip to Paris, a place her lover had always dreamed of visiting. Katie had another little surprise up her sleeve: "Whoever she takes will be asked (by my brother) to take her to the top of the Eiffel Tower and give her a letter that I've written. I had a lot of fun writing the letter and planning the trip. I can't tell you how excited she's going to be when she opens the letter addressed to "My one and only true love."

Whenever I have helped my clients plan their *Future Surprises*, I've always been impressed by the creativity and the amount of love they have put into organizing these gifts. It might seem like an unreasonable amount of effort, but really it's not dissimilar to any other occasion when for some reason you are unable to make the party, because of work commitments, travel complications or because you live too far away. In this instance, at the very least, you might arrange for a small gift to be delivered, but if it were a special occasion, you'd probably go to a lot more trouble to compensate for your absence at the event.

One last example comes from a couple, who, like Roger, had no immediate concerns about their health. They were both active in the services and were often away on assignment. They worried about the future of their teenage daughter should the "what if" happen to one, or God forbid, both of them. When I shared the idea of *Future Surprises* with them, they both got very excited. The couple had a great marriage, founded in part by their similar interests and line of work. They hoped their daughter would eventually find someone she loved as deeply, and when that happened, they wanted her wedding to be a very special day. Once they'd heard about the *Future Surprise* concept, they came up with a great idea: "We could do something special for her wedding day. Let's arrange a fund to buy her dress, and then, even if we're still here, it will already be paid for when the day comes. Either way, she'll have a treat coming her way." The couple chatted on, the wife making the point that, "I want her to have more than a dress, we need something meaningful, something lasting, a special something from each of us, I don't know what though . . . "

We talked for a while longer, and I shared some of the examples that my other clients had proposed. Then it came to her, "A locket. With a picture of us inside, and an inscription on the outside. A few words. A blessing for their marriage!" I don't know if this couple went on to create their *Future Surprise*, but judging by the level of excitement they shared, my guess is they did. It seemed such a lovely gift, and the idea alone seemed to alleviate their feelings of guilt surrounding their high-risk profession. Creating a *Future Surprise* gave them the opportunity to prepare, just in case the worst should ever happen. Perhaps you can draw inspiration from this couple, or use the following ideas to help you decide what *Future Surprise* you will create for your survivors:

❋ Jewelry, which can easily be engraved to hold a message or photograph, perhaps a locket or a watch.

❀ A letter, preferably hand-written on beautiful stationery or a series of cards.

❀ A song, performed by a band, or recorded and delivered on CD/MP3.

❀ Flowers on birthdays, anniversaries and Valentine's.

❀ Trees or a plant, something that will continue to grow every year, always reminding them of you.

❀ Set up a fund for an important event: college, a wedding, the purchase of a first home, or even a holiday.

❀ A video or series of photographs with a loving message recorded from you for their special day.

❀ A speech that someone else will read to them, perhaps for a wedding, graduation or other special day.

❀ A stocking, which will be warmly welcomed, especially if this is a Christmas tradition for your family.

❀ Your secret family recipe collection.

If your imagination has not been sparked, then I suggest you watch the films *P.S. I Love You* and *The Ultimate Gift*, or go to the Recommended Viewing section at the back of this book. You will find a list of films that will give you a better idea of how to help your survivors through the difficult "firsts." Just remember that whatever you choose to do, it will undoubtedly convey the one thing your loved ones really want to hear—wrapped up in your surprise will be the tender message that you did, and still do really care.

7

Life Story

Knowing our past, we shall find strength and wisdom to
meet the present — Gertrude Weil, Political Campaigner

It's a family vacation has arrived, and everyone's gathered together, chatting over a bowl of peanuts and some beers. Uncle
Bob starts telling the tale about how he wooed Aunt Mary from
the window of his parents' caravan with a bottle of cheap wine
and a line of Shakespeare. Eyes roll in despair. Then Mom pipes
up, "Do you remember that time when George was little, and he
walked over to the neighbor's wearing nothing but his father's
oversized shoes?" This results in cries of "Nooooo! Mooomm,
shut-up!" from a very embarrassed teenage George.

Not everyone understands the value of such family trivia and one
day, years from now, these people—your children, grandchildren
or even their children—will wish that Uncle Bob and Mom were
still around to share those stories. Such amusing and interesting
insights into the lives of parents, grandparents and great grand-

parents add color and depth to the family history. One day your survivors will wish they knew so much more about you, and how the choices you made influenced the person that they've become. Your *Life Story* will help them to appreciate why they think, talk, behave, and believe the things they do.

Share Your Lessons and Words of Wisdom

Storytelling is something we've done since the beginning of time. We wouldn't have progressed very far if the elders hadn't shared their lessons and words of wisdom with the younger ones. Passing on knowledge from one generation to another has been vital for our evolution. Yet we no longer place such importance on the transfer of stories from the older to the younger generation. In our youth-focused, fast-paced culture, it's no longer a priority. The knowledge of our seniors is all too often discounted and branded as worthless, irrelevant, and old-fashioned.

This is the kind of belief that gets us into trouble because we miss out on the many benefits of this tradition, which exist both for those imparting their wisdom and those who are listening. When younger audiences learn about those who came before them, they gain a sense of context, a framework of reference and a foundation for understanding why things are the way they are. The elders, the ones sharing their knowledge or telling their story, benefit from the therapeutic effect of reminiscing, which can help them to find meaning in their experiences and a sense of completion in the events that have constituted their life.

Stories are also a powerful tool for teaching others a specific skill, which can help the younger generation to gain the wisdom needed to maneuver through the world. All too often, the younger ones are left to learn the hard way, working things out for themselves, through personal and often painful experience. But it doesn't have to be that way. They could benefit from learning about your experiences and the mistakes you've already made. You are older and wiser. You have learned how to make better life choices. You've discovered values that make life easier. This knowledge can put your loved ones on the fast track to a happier and more successful life. Remember how Bob did this in the film *My Life*, by sharing the skills he had learned with his son, teaching him to make spaghetti, jump-start a car and how to give a good hand shake.

Like Bob, each of us can share our acquired wisdom, the knowledge we've gained from our professions, the hobbies we've enjoyed, not to mention the cultural and social developments that have happened during our lifetime. By sharing stories about our families, religion, rituals and traditions we can help our survivors gain a better understanding of their own history, their personal lives and their relationships. This can also help to reinforce the loving bond and memories of the times they shared with you. It will encourage them to appreciate how the achievements of generations before them have influenced who they've become today. Armed with this information, they'll find it easier to connect with and maintain the traditions or rituals that have been passed down through the generations of your family or community. This will help to give them a sense of belonging and continuity, which will in turn help them feel more connected to a wider, wiser, and well-established community, especially when they are suffering from the sense of isolation that commonly comes with bereavement.

Don't think for a moment that your surviving family won't appreciate your *Life Story* just because they don't request this information today. When you are no longer here, even teenage George will wish he could spend an afternoon reminiscing about his escapades in those over-sized shoes! We all share an innate desire to connect with our past. We want to know about our families — who they were, what they liked or disliked, where they worked, what they believed in, what they learned and what motivated them. In the *Allianz American Legacies Study* mentioned in Chapter Two, the researchers found that the request for "'values and life lessons" didn't come from the elders (as you might imagine), but rather from the adult children participating in the study. Of these, 75% said that they wanted the memoirs and wisdom of their parents as part of their ongoing legacy. What they didn't necessarily appreciate about this request was how the act of sharing stories and life lessons would also help their parents. A common cause of suffering for the elderly, and people who are approaching the end-of-life, is their belief that their life seems to have been wasted or had little meaning. Dr. Christina Puchalski, pioneer and internationally recognized expert in the integration of spirituality into healthcare, observes in her enlightening book, *A Time for Listening and Caring*, "Meaning and purpose are things that all people seek; the inability to find that meaning and purpose can lead to depression and anxiety." When we reach the end, the need for completion is magnified, forcing us to look back and ask:

✳ What was I here for?

✳ What difference did I make?

✳ What was the point of my existence?

✳ What has been important to me?

✳ What have I learned?

We want to know the answers. If we can't make sense of our own existence, then life can seem worthless, and we suffer, both spiritually and emotionally. Our life has to mean something. While working with people who are coming to terms with their departure, Dr. Puchalski often finds that: "The most common spiritual themes include lack of meaning and purpose in life, hopelessness, despair, guilt or shame, lack of connection with others or with God, anger at God or others and a sense of abandonment by God or others." We need to find this deeper meaning and know that we have been of value if we are to avoid unnecessary suffering and find peace in our final days. How can this be achieved? The solution, it seems, is something we already possess, as gerontologists Gary Kenyon and William Randell describe in *Restorying Our Lives: Personal Growth Through Autobiographical Reflection.* "Ultimately, the richest resource for meaning and healing is one we already possess. It rests (mostly untapped) in the material of our own *Life Story*, in the sprawling, many-layered *text* that has been accumulating within us across the years, weaving itself in the depths of, and as, our life."

To Complete the Circle of Life

By reflecting on our experiences, values, and the lessons we've learned we can find deeper meaning in our lives, but it is not until we have shared this knowledge with others that we can complete the circle of life. As you look back on the events of your life, you might notice that even the tough times, when you struggled and suffered, weren't actually so bad. Somehow, these challenges helped you open another door, forcing you to grow, or they helped you to develop a deeper faith or gave you strength in an area where previously there was none. As you relay your *Life Story*, you might see how you weren't really the victim of circumstance, but rather, how some of it was your own responsibility. Or, as you consider whether your life has been of any importance and wonder if anyone will remember you, you'll see how even the smiles you shared made a difference to someone's day.

This act of reflecting and sharing your achievements, the victories and the losses, the knowledge you've gained, the places you've seen and the contribution you've made is how you go about creating your *Life Story*. In doing this, you will bring meaning to the events that have comprised this unique experience that has been your life. As you think about how to pass on the lessons you have learned, you'll realize that what you lost, or gained, can now be of benefit to someone else. When you see that your experiences—no matter how big or small—can actually serve someone else, you'll realize something very important: that no matter what mistakes, regrets or disappointments you've had along the way, to someone, your life will always be precious.

Most of our life experiences will have been captured in some way: within us as feelings or memories, or recorded in the form of letters, journals, documents, poems and diaries. One day these will be of great interest to your surviving family. It's important that you keep these safe so they can be incorporated into *Your Legacy of Love*. Please don't let them go undiscovered, lost in storage, your basement, or the deep recesses of your mind! You might, of course, feel uncomfortable about the idea of someone rooting through your memoirs and private affairs. Try to appreciate how these treasures will bring immense joy to your loved ones and realize that by the time they get their hands on them, the potential for embarrassment will have disappeared.

After discovering Mom's diaries, my brother and his fiancée snuggled up on a winter's night to learn about the not-so-innocent escapades of her late teenage years. Had Mom known that they were reading about how she'd been "kissed profusely" by an attractive young man, I'm sure her cheeks would have glowed bright red. But, had she censored this information for fear of future embarrassment, or worse, destroyed it, Jacob's wife-to-be would never have been able to get to know the woman who would have become her mother-in-law. Many years from now this could be your grandchildren, sitting down to read about the exploits of their grandparents Mary and Bob. Just think of all the fun they'll have!

Obviously, diaries are not the only medium for sharing your *Life Story* or lessons. However, they do give a very honest and personal insight into the life of their creator, which makes them difficult to censor. If you are worried about sharing certain episodes of your life, or there is a skeleton you'd rather keep in the closet, then it might be better to share your stories and lessons in another form using something that enables you to edit anything you wish to keep private. Instead, you could write your *Life Story* as an autobiography or tell it as a series of short stories. You could also record your lessons on camera and create a series of short films or videos in the style of a documentary.

Let's Hear It! Tell Your Tales

There are so many ways to tell your tales. If you are artistically inclined, then a scrapbook, photobook or montage might be a better way to go, and if you are particularly talented, then you could even draw a series of cartoons or paintings. Mediums I typically use to help others share their *Life Story* and lessons are:

❋	Short Stories	❋	Journals
❋	Cartoons	❋	Paintings
❋	Collages	❋	Poetry
❋	Films	❋	Photobooks
❋	Autobiographies	❋	Scrapbooks
❋	Memoirs	❋	Websites
❋	Audio Recordings	❋	Plays

Don't think you can't start this now, just because the *D-Word* seems so far away. Many people record little bits of their *Life Story* as they go along, capturing the lessons and major events that hold special memories on video and in photographs. They often do this because they're concerned that their memory will fail and the things they've experienced will be reduced to a muddled haze. This is a smart thing to do because, as you age, or develop an illness, it will become harder to recall your story as debilitating symptoms may prevent you from recalling or communicating clearly.

Before you start preparing your *Life Story*, think about the time and resources you have available to you, and what format is best suited to your surviving family. If you have very young children, an inspirational story or a book of short stories could work well, but if your family is grown up, an autobiographical style might be more appropriate. You could use chronological chapters to detail the most important events or experiences: The Early Years, Your Education, Your Wedding Day, Life Before the Children . . . and so on. You could even add illustrations and photographs —that picture of you as a teenager with the terrible haircut and ever-so fashionable outfit is guaranteed to get some laughs! Gaining different perspectives on your *Life Story* from other family members will add greater depth to your gift. Take a pen and paper, recording device or video, and interview your relatives, colleagues and friends. Some might be a little reticent at first, but once you get them started there will be no stopping them. Everyone loves to share a good story, especially over a Coke or a cold beer!

If you have written a memoir or autobiography, you will want to have it printed, rather than leave it buried under a pile of dusty folders. Various print-on-demand facilities, known as POD printing, now exist, and you can use these to have a single book printed at very low cost. You can also create a photobook using software like Apple's iPhoto, or one of the many online photobook services such as Inkubook or Shutterfly. Just type the names into the search engine Google and you'll find one that suits you.

Alternatively, you could save your stories and photographs onto a CD or DVD and distribute them to family and friends as one of your *Future Surprises*. If you don't really see yourself as much of a writer, you could always hire someone to help ghostwrite your *Life Story*. There are a number of media organizations who will come and interview you, capturing your lessons and words of wisdom on video—a list of these organizations can be found in the Recommended Websites section at the back of this book, or on: *www.realizethegift.com*

You could also take inspiration from Becky Williamson, a British teenager who died from lung cancer, leaving behind her beloved three-year-old daughter Courtney. Becky believed that her daughter, like all children, should know who her mother was, what she had believed in, and most importantly, just how deeply her mother loved her and how sorry she was that she was missing the opportunity to see her daughter grow up. In the early stages of her cancer, Becky started filming her life with Courtney; she shot over one hundred hours of film, creating a beautiful gift of her *Life Story*, something that Courtney will surely treasure as she watches it in the years to come.

Whatever medium you decide to use, make sure that the "voice" you record is your own. It's quite common for people to impersonate the voice of someone else when they first attempt to express themselves in this way. We often do this to protect ourselves, or gain acceptance, but your loved ones won't want to hear the voice of a stranger. It will help if you write or talk as though you're having a conversation with someone that you love and trust; this way your "voice" will sound authentic. Picture the person who will receive your *Life Story* and lessons, imagine you're talking to them face-to-face with your normal "voice"—it's the one they'll want to hear, over and over again. After all this hard work, you'll want to make sure that your *Life Story* is preserved and delivered to the intended recipient, so leave it with a trustworthy individual, your lawyer, mentor, or a good friend.

You may, for some reason, think that you're too old to tell your *Life Story*. If that is the case, then take note of an experience I had with my Granny Hambly. Granny had just been diagnosed with breast cancer. She was at the grand old age of ninety-four so I knew there wasn't much time left. When I went to visit, I was prepared; my bag was packed with pens, notebook and a camera videophone. We sat down over a cup of tea and I asked Granny if she would share her *Life Story*. She agreed. Over the next two days, I asked her countless questions about her life and we talked until we were blue in the face. She shared everything, from her first kiss, to the grief she'd experienced over the deaths of her dear husband and her daughter, my mother. These conversations had us in fits of laughter and mopping up the tears. We talked about her first job and Australia, the country she had left at twenty-six to "follow her bliss" sailing on the Oriana for six weeks so she could marry my grandfather, her beloved English gentleman.

She told me how much she'd loved to play music—yet in all the time I'd known her, I never saw her play an instrument or listen to anything other than the news on the radio. This prompted me to find some classical music, something she said she'd always enjoyed, and a CD player. A few seconds into track one, I noticed that there was a magic twinkle in her faded blue eyes. When the CD ended, I asked if she wanted it switched off, she answered, "No! I'd like it to play again." And so it did. Quietly and continuously in the background, all through that night and the next day, right up until she passed away the following day. I am so grateful we had that time together to put her stories onto paper. Since then I've interviewed most of my family members, with the aim of recording the remainder of my family history, before it's too late. I'm sure that in years to come, my children, grandchildren, and great-grandchildren will enjoy these bedtime stories, particularly the one of Granny Hambly and how she sailed for six weeks across the oceans to be with the man she loved. Don't you think that if my ninety-four--year-old grandmother can create her *Life Story*, then you can too?

To Answer The Vital Questions

Now that you know how to leave your *Life Story,* you are probably wondering what you should actually share and what your surviving loved ones will want to hear. Your entire story could take up more than a few shelves of the central library, so I suggest you keep it to the core themes and identify the interesting bits before you start. Your *Life Story* and lessons can, of course, include anything you choose, but ideally you should select subjects that convey some kind of personal insight into family ancestry, culture or tradition, and the lessons you've learned along the way. Give some thought to the insights that might help your survivors make better life choices, especially your children. Remember there is no set formula for *Your Legacy of Love*; just do what feels right for you. Just in case you find this exercise challenging, I've compiled a list of vital questions that you can answer to easily create your *Life Story*. You can use these as a guide or have someone interview you, after all, no one knows more about your life than you! Alternatively, you could answer the questions in a journal and then gift it as a *Future Surprise* for your survivors. So, let's hear it!

❋ What are the most memorable moments or events in your life, and what did you learn from them?

❋ Who has been your hero and why?

❋ What values have you gained from your friends and family?

❋ What traditions or rituals are important in your family and why?

❋ Who is your best friend and why?

❋ What have you learned about love and forgiveness?

❋ What are the most important lessons you have learned about money?

❋ What is your greatest achievement?

❋ What historical events had the most influence during your lifetime?

❋ What changes have you seen in the world that you are happiest about?

❋ What was your chosen career path and why did you pick this one?

❋ How have you fulfilled your professional goals and aspirations?

❋ What has been your greatest creative achievement?

❋ How have your spiritual beliefs supported you throughout your life, especially during the tough times?

✷ What three qualities do you value most in others?

✷ What are the greatest lessons you've learned from someone else?

✷ Which of your personality traits have been the most difficult to accept during your lifetime?

✷ Have you made any major mistakes or bad decisions, and if so, how did you cope with these?

✷ Have you traveled abroad? If so, what did you gain from experiencing this different culture?

✷ What are the three most important lessons a young person might learn from the way you have lived your life?

✷ What have you loved about yourself and your life?

✷ What gifts have you been able to offer, professionally and personally?

✷ How has your life been remarkable?

✷ How will you live on through your legacy?

8

Musical Memories

*Music expresses that which cannot be said and on which it is
impossible to be silent — Victor Hugo, French Poet*

I've always been amazed at how a few lines of song can instantly
alter my mood, transporting me from a sad and sorry state into one
of foot-tapping joy! Whether it is a simple tune or a full orchestral
ensemble, music has the power to transform our moods, igniting
strong emotional responses in us all—fear, excitement, laughter,
tears and a deep sense of peace. Just observe teenagers as they get
a quick fix of MTV, seeking relief from adolescent angst. Music
is like a mind-altering drug—and many develop a life-long ad-
diction.

This might explain why, according to industry reports, we spent
over $17 billion on music last year and why we actually bought
more music than we did prescription drugs! There might be a
legitimate reason for this. Unlike most pharmaceutical or recre-

ational drugs, the effects of using music are rarely detrimental, even when mainlining the stuff through iPods! In fact, according to musicologists, neuroscientists, musicians and psychologists, certain types of music can actually have a positive impact on our mental and physical health. Music can influence the body, mind, emotions and behaviors in a therapeutic way. This power of persuasion is frequently put into effect by therapists and organizations that use a prescription of song to soothe, stimulate or motivate us and our surroundings—an area where the entertainment industry leads the way. Recognizing that the correct combination of sound and celluloid is central to the success of any film, directors work closely with composers, carefully corresponding every note and scene to ensure the audience will have a specific emotional response. When the two are not in sync, the film can take on a totally different meaning.

Listen Up! The Power of Sound

Do you remember Leonardo DiCaprio and Kate Winslet perched on the ship's bow in James Cameron's epic film, *Titanic*, when Rose tenderly kisses Jack's hand? Now, what if the sound track to the closing credits—Celine Dion's, "My Heart Will Go On"— was replaced with Coldplay's, "Don't Panic" wouldn't the romance quickly evaporate? Not convinced? Then try watching *Jaws* with the sound switched off. Without John Williams' legendary composition 'da...dun, da...dun'—you'll find that the sequence of a rubber fin emerging from the deep generates mild amusement rather than Spielberg's intended sense of dread. Some companies have spent millions seeking a better understanding of the power in musical sway.

One fast-food giant invested a considerable sum to study the effect of music on their customers' behaviors. They discovered that food consumption was dramatically altered according to the pace of the music that was being played in the restaurant. (The next time you're in line for a burger, don't be surprised when the mellow background music is replaced with an up-tempo dance track, persuading diners to swiftly scoff their food, quickly clearing the tables for other customers!) Some organizations, like the London Underground, have been familiar with the infectious capacity of music to effect mood and behavior for quite some time. During the Second World War, under instruction from the British Government, uplifting classical music was played at various stations to boost the morale of the many civilians who were sheltering there from the bombings.

It's incredible how quickly music can brighten us from our shades of gray. No one is immune. Weighed down by the woes of humanity, feeling nothing but misery, we've all tried to escape with

a song. Only a few minutes later we're in tears, the music having triggered a release, freeing us from the pent-up suffering that
we've been holding in. Some use music to self-medicate, perhaps
after a really bad break-up or some other disappointing news.
They'll swallow a dose of uplifting dance music, something like
Chic's song '"Everybody Dance":

Music never lets you down,
Puts a smile on your face,
Anytime, any place.
Dancing helps relieve the pain,
Soothes your mind,
Makes you happy again.

An upbeat song like this can help us to remember there is a bright-
er side to life. As we're bopping away to the motivating beat, we
realize that the bad news doesn't seem quite so bad and somehow we'll bounce back. Most of us are intuitively aware of these
motivating properties inherent to music but we don't necessarily
understand why a certain song puts us back in "sync."

Will Soothe Their Suffering

In the past hundred years, scientists, psychologists, neuroscientists and musicologists have converged to study an area known as Music Therapy, uncovering the reasons why "music soothes our mind, and makes us happy again." Their work is based on the discoveries of Pythagoras, who is credited as the founding father of musical medicine. Pythagoras both practiced and taught at the Ancient Mystery Schools in Delphi, Greece around 500 BC. He taught students how the correct sequence of chords or melodies played on a musical instrument could produce a specific response within the human organism that accelerated the healing process, by impacting the brainwaves, respiration and the heartbeat, thus transforming the health of the patient.

A few thousand years later, Dutch scientist Christian Huygens identified this as a universal principle of physics, which became known as "entrainment". The law of entrainment refers to the synchronization of one or more objects because the vibration of one is stronger than the other; this means they move naturally from one state (disharmony) to another (harmony). Huygens stumbled across this phenomenon while working on the design of a pendulum clock. He noticed that when a number of grandfather clocks are placed together, their pendulums begin by swinging at different rates, yet within a few hours all the pendulums are swinging at exactly the same speed. This is what happens when we hear certain sounds or listen to a piece of music with a strong beat, which stimulates the brainwaves to resonate, resulting in sharper concentration and more alert thinking. A slower tempo will promote a calm, or meditative state. That is why, when a certain song blasts from the radio we're transported so easily from a miserable mood into a more divine disposition. This also explains why music with inspiring lyrics can motivate and stimulate higher states of consciousness, such as courage or creativity, while a tune with a gentle melody can help us to relax, become calmer and more peaceful. This process is also known as the ISO principle, something that music therapists and musicologists use (just like Pythagoras) to positively impact the mental and physical health of their patients, helping them to:

❋ Release pent-up or unexpressed feelings.

❋ Transform negative emotions into positive ones.

❋ Shift into a state of liveliness or serenity.

According to Dr. Tomas Chamorro-Premuzic, senior researcher at Goldsmiths College, London, "Every individual, even the most unmusical, is likely to be touched by music if they choose the right song." The findings of his extensive research into the way we use music for emotional regulation, such as a pick-me-up after a hard day or as a cognitive learning tool, have been published in the *British Journal of Psychology* and *Psychology Today Magazine*. The American Music Therapy Association reports that patients suffering from grief and depression respond well to Music Therapy, with significant psychological and physical health improvements essential to healthy recovery from grief, including:

❋ A reduction in stress and stress-related symptoms.

❋ Enhanced memory function.

❋ Improved communication.

❋ The ability to better express feelings.

❋ Elevation in moods and feeling of well-being.

❋ Improved creativity and self-expression.

❋ Reduction in emotional and physical pain.

It is especially important for survivors to express and release the negative feelings of fear, anger, jealousy, blame, regret, hatred and guilt that frequently arise during the *Reaction* and *Reflection* phases of grief. These emotions often get bottled up for fear of upsetting someone or because they are frightened of sharing such a deep part of themselves with another person. When these emotions are repressed they can manifest later as physical, mental or psychological problems, which can easily tip the bereaved into the *Danger Zone* of unresolved grief or abnormal grief. That's where music can come into play, as a tool to release the cap on this emotional bottle. Like a film director, you can select a piece of music or a song to motivate the moods and health of your audience—your surviving loved ones. By incorporating music into *Your Legacy of Love* you can soothe your survivors from afar, encouraging the free expression of their emotions and reducing both their suffering and the chances of developing major health concerns.

Music can also help your survivors maintain their connection with you. As the years go by, treasured memories slowly begin to fade, but music can help them to record, preserve and recall the precious moments they spent with you. I'm sure you've had the experience of listening to a familiar song and being instantly transported back to the moment in time that you most strongly associated with that song. Immediately your senses are flooded with the images, smells and sensations of that day, like the time when you finally got together with someone you adored. Remember how you danced together in a close embrace, perhaps a classic Barry White love song playing in the background, with moonlight streaming through the window, as you waltzed back and forth and pictured your future together?

Keep Memories Alive

Now, fast-forward thirty years. In the time that's passed, you got married, had children and were on the path to Happy Ever After. Then things got tough. You've been fighting and struggling to make things work, asking yourself, "Can we really see this through, or is it time to let each other go?" Then, one day as you're going about your business, the "speakers-that-be" seem to engage in a musical conspiracy. Everywhere you go, in the gas station, the supermarket, even the doctors' waiting room, *that* song is playing. The vivid memories of that first night together flood your mind—the outfits you were wearing, their seductive scent, the lustful whisperings you shared and the feeling of holding hands tightly, as the two of you slowly sauntered home. As you picture that first embrace, you are reminded of all the reasons why you fell in love, your heart skips a beat and a smile grows on your face as you realize that you could never walk away from all that history. You make a decision to be more forgiving and to frequently use *that* song as your medicine.

It's incredible how a song can easily trigger memories, but without such a prompt, often they are more difficult to recall. This loss of memory is something that will challenge your survivors as time takes its toll, and those once-clear memories of your familiar features—your idiosyncrasies and expressions of love—will become harder and harder to recall. Time is a great healer, but it can also be a destructive force, erasing many of the essential threads that keep your loved ones, especially young children, connected to you. This can be extremely frustrating and distressing for the bereaved. Losing knowledge that comprises such a vital component of their own history, relationships, and family, can seriously erode their sense of belonging. Bereaved children suffer from this much more than adults, because the time to form memories and develop their relationship with you might have been brief. When a parent, sibling or grandparent dies, the connection to them can quickly become tenuous unless something is done to strengthen and maintain this bond. With *Musical Memories* you can help your loved ones safeguard this all-important information and promote the recall of those precious memories.

I first stumbled upon the idea of *Musical Memories* after creating a thank-you present for my Mom. My twenty-first birthday was fast approaching, and knowing that this would probably be the last celebration we would share together, Mom was organizing a big party. Despite the illness she invested considerable energy into the preparations and this left me wondering how I could ever thank her; not only for arranging the party, but for everything she had given me during those twenty-one years. A present just wasn't enough. I wanted to share my gratitude and faith in her, to show how much I'd been inspired by her battle against cancer and to say that I was truly honored to be her daughter.

After a few days of unsuccessful searching, I remember thinking, "Perhaps a song might be appropriate?" For the next few days, I trawled through my friends' music collections, searching for something with just the right lyrics, but nothing seemed to fit. Then, one morning, while listening to the radio, there it was. The words touched something deep inside my heart and I knew it said everything I wanted to, but didn't know how. I asked my girl-friend Sarah if she would sing the chosen song on the day of the party. Thankfully she kindly and willingly agreed.

With fifty of our closest friends and family members gathered around, the food gone, and everyone in a buoyant mood—thanks to my uncle's generous servings of wine and champagne—it was time to deliver my gift. The room was silenced. I addressed Mom, who was sitting diagonally across from me: "Mom, I am so grateful for the loving presence you have provided in my life. You have been a wonderful role model: campaigning for what you believe in, fighting against the odds. Thank you for always being there, despite the challenges I presented in my teens! I can never thank you enough for everything that you've done for me. Here is my gift to you. An expression of my gratitude and the faith I have in you." Then Sarah appeared on stage and began her solo performance, backed by the acoustic version of Mariah Carey's, "Hero," she sang:

And then a hero comes along,
With the strength to carry on,
And you cast your fears aside,
And you know you can survive,
So when you feel like hope is gone,
Look inside you and be strong,
And you'll finally see the truth,
That a hero lies in you.

I was engulfed by waves of sadness and a sense of defeat because I knew that Mom would not survive, and soon we would be saying our final farewells. Tears ran down my face. As I looked around, I realized I wasn't alone; there was hardly a dry eye in the room. As the song ended, and the applause began, I walked across the room to hug my very own "hero." Our wet faces pressing tightly together, she whispered to me, "Thank you, darling. I love you so much, don't ever forget that." Now, whenever I hear "Hero" playing, the lyrics steal me away from the task in hand, as my senses are filled with wonderfully clear memories of that day. It's as though I'm back in her arms. I see her wide green eyes brimming with tears and feel the warmth of her embrace. This always brings a smile to my face as I'm reminded of the comfort I always felt in her presence. Thankfully, because of the *Musical Memories* we'd created with that song, the precious memories of that day will remain with me forevermore.

Motivate Their Moods

As time has gone on, I have realized that the songs we listened to as a family motivated us on a subconscious level. Mom loved to sing, especially on long car journeys, although it was something we really hated as teenagers. Subjected to lengthy renditions of songs from the musicals *Cats*, *South Pacific* and *The Sound of Music*, we made fun of her with fingers firmly stuck in our ears! Perhaps that's why at the time I didn't notice the message hidden in Mom's favorite songs. I certainly didn't appreciate the powerful impact they would later have on me. To my surprise, the famous *South Pacific* chant, "I'm Gonna Wash That Man Right Outta' My Hair" has stayed with me, serving as a reminder of my own strength and helping me recover from several heartbreaks!

I've also found that "Climb Every Mountain," the anthem from *The Sound of Music*, has lifted my spirits, even when the vice-like grip of grief had me convinced that things couldn't possibly improve. Even though I didn't receive a *Legacy of Love* from Mom, the music she listened to has definitely continued to motivate my moods. This is something you can do too, selecting songs with motivating lyrics to help your survivors move from the negative states of grief towards the healing states of joy, hope and inspiration. Just think how a song with the right lyrics could remind them that "Things Will Only Get Better," or to "Always Look on the Bright Side of Life!"

You can create a compilation of songs by purchasing music from an online source like Apple's iTunes store, and then record these onto a CD or save them as a playlist for iPods or mp3 players (you will, of course, need to make sure that this is not an infringement of copyright laws). You can also buy the single or album of your chosen song(s) from any music store. If you happen to be musically talented, you could write your own lyrics and record your own song, leaving it as a *Future Surprise* for a special birthday, anniversary or important event, like a wedding or graduation. Alternatively, you could hire a band to perform the song of your choice.

Whatever method you choose for your *Musical Memories*, take care to select songs that have an appropriate message, as what might seem welcoming to one person's ears can be deafening to another. Pay attention to the music that influences or soothes the mood of your loved ones and listen carefully to the lyrics of any song you wish to use. It's important to think about how your audience will interpret the song, as they are most likely to consider this your final message to them. Picking the right music isn't as easy as it might seem. "Many years of research have shown me that there is no set prescription, no particular piece of music that will make everyone feel better or more relaxed," says Suzanne Hanser, chairperson of the music therapy department at Berklee College of Music in Boston. She adds, "What counts is familiarity, musical taste, and the kinds of memories, feelings, and associations a piece of music brings to mind. Some people relax to classical music, others like the Moody Blues. The key is to individualize your musical selections." To ensure your musical choices hit the right note, ask these questions about the song(s) you are thinking of using:

❋ What is your intention for this song?

❋ What is the best medium to present this song?

❋ What music style does your audience prefer?

❋ How will this piece of music connect them to you?

❋ Will this song bring back sweet or bitter memories?

❋ Is this piece of music special to them or you?

❋ How might this piece of music motivate them?

❋ Will the lyrics elevate or depress them?

❋ How might this song affect their self-esteem?

❋ Will the lyrics help them release blocked emotions?

Picking songs for your *Musical Memories* will probably be easier because this is very personal, but finding music to motivate moods can be a little trickier. There are so many songs to choose from, it's hard to know which ones will heal, soothe or motivate. To simplify matters, I've compiled a Top Ten list of songs that I've found to be effective. Don't worry if you are struggling to find the right songs, just borrow one from this selection:

The Top Ten

❀ The smoky tones of Nat King Cole's classic "Unforgettable" is ideal for reminding a long-term partner that no matter where you are, they will "always be forever in your heart."

❀ R. Kelly's uplifting song "I Believe I Can Fly" contains an empowering message that could inspire confidence and self-esteem in all age groups.

❀ Rod Stewart's "Forever Young" conveys the gentle message that you will always have faith in them.

❀ "There's Always Someone Cooler Than You" by Ben Folds could help remind young listeners that they are just as intelligent, and attractive as the next person.

❀ Anger and resentment are common reactions to loss, especially if the cause is accidental. Lauryn Hill's song "Forgive Them Father" might be the perfect antidote.

❀ Christina Aguilera's song "The Voice Within" suggests that a young woman should trust her own intuition, which is an empowering message to share with a daughter or girlfriend.

❋ "Shout" by Tears for Fears could really encourage your survivors to release their emotions—best played at full volume while driving in the car, alone!

❋ One song from Collective Soul asks the most important question of your survivors, "How Do You Love?"

❋ The popular show-tune "You'll Never Walk Alone" originally written for the musical Carousel is ideal for any audience, reminding them to keep hope in their hearts and to hold their heads up high.

❋ Joe Cocker's song "You Are So Beautiful" doesn't require much explanation, but it will make a welcome gift for any woman in your life.

PART III

✽✽✽✽✽✽✽✽✽✽✽✽✽✽✽✽✽✽✽✽✽✽✽✽✽

. . . in Goodbye

✽✽✽✽✽✽✽✽✽✽✽✽✽✽✽✽✽✽✽✽✽✽✽✽✽

9

Define Your Wishes

Death never takes a wise man by surprise; he is always ready
to go — Jean de la Fontaine, French Poet and Writer

Have you noticed how everything comes with a disclaimer these
days, this book included? The intention behind these stipulations,
often filled with ominous warnings, isn't, as it often seems, to
absolve the company or individual who is offering the service of
responsibility. Rather, it's to protect you, the end-user. The aim
of disclaimers is primarily to make you aware of the limitations
of the service, the possible risks, and the potential for physical or
emotional harm that may occur as a result of using it. Invariably,
this is a good thing and having access to this information allows
you to make an informed decision, so that you can reduce the
chances of an unexpected or undesirable experience occurring. If
only we were issued with a disclaimer when we arrived here for
this thing called Life. It might read something like this:

i) IMPORTANT! ENTER AT YOUR OWN RISK. USE ONLY AS DIRECTED. NO MONEY DOWN, NO PURCHASE NECESSARY. YOU ASSUME FULL RESPONSIBILITY. ANY ACTIONS OR INACTIONS DURING THIS LIFE CANNOT BE BLAMED ON ANYONE OTHER THAN YOURSELF.

ii) YOU AGREE TO TAKE RESPONSIBILITY FOR ANY DIRECT, INDIRECT, INCIDENTAL OR CONSEQUENTIAL DAMAGES RESULTING FROM ANY DEFECT, ERROR OR FAILURE TO PERFORM DURING THIS LIFE.

iii) YOU ASSUME RESPONSIBILITY FOR THE PHYSICAL CONDITION OF YOUR BODY IN THIS LIFE. ORDINARY WEAR AND TEAR SHOULD BE EXPECTED. IF A FAILURE TO MAINTAIN YOUR BODY PREVENTS YOU FROM COMPLETING THIS LIFE, WE ACCEPT NO LIABILITY, OTHER THAN IN SPECIAL CIRCUMSTANCES.

iv) SHOULD YOU REQUIRE ASSISTANCE IN ANY MATTER RELATING TO THIS LIFE, THEN CONSULT APPROPRIATE PROFESSIONALS AND FOLLOW THEIR ADVICE.

v) YOU ACKNOWLEDGE THAT THIS LIFE MAY BE TERMINATED AT ANY TIME, WITHOUT WARNING, BY AN ACT OF GOD, ACCIDENT, FORCE MAJEURE, AN ACT OF GOVERNMENTAL AGENCY OR PUBLIC ENEMY, OR THAT

YOUR LIFE WILL OTHERWISE EVENTUALLY EXPIRE. IN SUCH AN EVENT, YOU ASSUME NO LIABILITY FOR ANY KIND OF LOSS, INJURY, DELAY OR DAMAGE CAUSED TO ANOTHER PARTY WHO MAY BE AFFECTED BY THIS.

vi) YOU HEREBY ACKNOWLEDGE THAT THERE IS A STRONG POSSIBILITY THAT YOU OR ANOTHER PARTY MAY EXPERIENCE SOMETHING UNDESIRED, INCLUD-ING, BUT NOT LIMITED TO EMOTIONAL AND PHYSICAL DISTRESS, IF YOU FAIL TO TAKE FULL RESPONSIBILITY IN PLANNING AND PREPARING FOR THE TERMINATION OR EXPIRATION OF YOUR LIFE.

Whether we like it or not, we have a responsibility, not only to ourselves, but also to our loved ones. Unfortunately we don't always take this responsibility seriously. All too often, people fail to acknowledge advice, like the one given in the final clause (vi); so they don't prepare and they don't plan. Perhaps it's because they don't understand the impact that their termination will have on their family and friends, or maybe it's because they are still in fear of "it," and their concerns about what hides around the corner loom large. This behavior will, of course, leave your survivors in the dark—unsupported, uneducated and quite frankly, downright scared.

The Onus Is On You

Usually when faced with such a major transition, we prefer to be in the know. We research events beforehand so that we can make the best decisions and avoid making mistakes that might cost us, either financially, mentally, emotionally or physically. That's why, like eager Boy Scouts, we share such a universal motivation to "be prepared," devouring courses, leaflets, classes, instructional videos and books to help us get ready. Just type "planning for" births, weddings, retirement, divorce, moving home, a new job or starting a new business, into the search field for online book retailer Amazon.com, and you'll find thousands of titles listed for each one. However, if you enter "planning for loss" or "preparing for death" only a few will appear. This seems a bit odd when you consider that fifty-six million people had their Life contracts expire last year. "We are ill-prepared to deal with death. We receive more education about simple first-aid than we do about loss, death, divorce and emotional loss," state the authors of *The Grief Recovery Handbook*, John W. James and Russell Friedman.

Perhaps this explains why in a Gallup Poll more than 70 percent of Americans reported a fear of dying in pain, alone, or without the chance to say goodbye. They are not the only ones. Research carried out by UK charity Dignity in Dying reported that one in three Britons fear dying alone. But it wasn't always this way. In the not-so-distant past, most people died naturally at home, surrounded by family and friends. However, during the past one hundred years, the end-of-life has been outsourced to residential homes, hospitals and hospices, taking with it the opportunity to learn about the intricacies of this important transition in the intimacy of our own homes. We are, of course, in many ways grateful for such "progress," but it's important to recognize that we've lost something as a result of this convenience; the subject is now a mystery to most of us.

In the ancient past, people worked hard to prepare themselves for this journey, to give their loved ones the best conditions for departing this life, believing that the soul would undergo a reincarnation or resurrection, perhaps changing form or moving through one doorway into the next. From around 1600 BC, the Egyptians incorporated offerings of food, jewels, figurines and instructions into their funerals with the aim of helping their deceased overcome obstacles in the next world. Their guide to a Happy Afterlife included hymns, spells, passwords and clues to help the deceased secure entry into the Sekhet-Hetepet (Fields of Reeds) where he or she might seek protection from the gods and attain the blissful status of a Khu (immortal being). Initially carved onto the tombs, these guides were later written on scrolls and placed inside the sarcophagus. These became known as *The Egyptian Book of the Dead*, although the direct translation is "The Book of Coming (or going forth) by Day." The Christians went a step further. After being subjected to the horrors of the Black Death during the Middle

163

Ages, they created a guidebook offering advice on how to "die well," known as the *Ars Moriendi*, which literally translates as "The Art of Dying." Created around 1415, this book prescribed advice on the spiritual, physical, emotional and practical aspects of preparing for the end-of-life. The manual, originally written in Latin, was translated into the prominent Western languages and widely distributed to the public. Unfortunately, the wisdom of this great book has been lost and forgotten. However, this doesn't mean that we must remain uneducated and unprepared for the "what if" but it does mean that we must seek out a new way to approach this subject.

My advice is to follow in the footsteps of pioneering leaders. When preparing for a new journey or project, their primary aim is to minimize the risks for both themselves and their team. They anticipate, research, discuss and plan ahead for all possible eventualities, using education, clear communication and evaluation. These leaders meet those who have traveled a similar path, asking questions, and seeking ways to reduce the potential for injury or mistakes. They are motivated by the desire to identify the route that will improve their chance of a successful, comfortable and safe journey. They understand that such a venture relies on discussions, so members can share their knowledge, fears and ideas, while plans can be reviewed, guidelines developed and the most suitable course of action established and agreed upon. Then, when the leader feels confident they've done their best to prepare for whatever lies ahead, they can begin with a certain peace of mind. When it comes to preparing for the "what if," a time when you'll be embarking on a journey into an unknown world, putting your life into the hands of others, won't you, like these leaders, want to know the risks and potential pitfalls? Won't you want to know your options? Which team member can be relied upon? Who you'd want to accompany you? What you can do to improve your comfort? It's easy to leave these things for the day when it demands your attention, but this can cause a lot of stress, both for you and your loved ones. Perhaps we should pay heed to the advice of the Dalai Lama, who writes in the foreword of Sogyal Rinpoche's classic bestseller, *The Tibetan Book of Living and Dying*: "We can either choose to ignore it or we can confront the prospect of our own death and by thinking clearly about it try to minimize the suffering that it can bring." What will you choose: To prepare for this journey as a pioneering leader who seeks success on this journey for themselves and their team, or to remain a passive bystander, reacting to events as they unfold, allowing someone else to take the helm?

Pioneer or Passive Bystander

Those who confront "it" make a powerful choice. By making a comprehensive plan for their departure they choose to create the conditions for a peaceful and pleasant end, rather than take the risk of being subjected to the ebb and flow of indecision or the countless pressures of life's end. They realize that, "Dying is hard work," as Rev. Jennifer Block of the Zen Hospice Center, San Francisco, explains. "It's not a passive process. Death involves a biochemical, biological, physical, mental, emotional and spiritual process. With the trials of illness, and the journey towards death, patients are not in a state for taking on board anything new." When a person actually dies, it is a very gentle thing. However, what leads up to this moment, the preparation, the emotional and physical process of dying, can be distressing. Most people naturally assume that death itself is unpleasant, but really it's the emotional and spiritual suffering that comes before and during the event that poses a real challenge for everyone. Still, few of us do much to prepare for this journey unless there is a pressing need, perhaps sparked by the diagnosis of a terminal illness, or because we work in a profession where our lives are genuinely at risk.

By ignoring this advice or leaving any preparation until the last minute, we take a massive risk. If, for example, we wait for the diagnosis of an illness or until we reach old age, there's a high probability that we will be too overwhelmed with pressures to make good decisions. Suddenly we will be racing against the clock with emotions running high and fears overpowering our ability to clearly express ourselves. Then there are the physical strains of illness, which can seriously affect the mind and body, making coherency difficult, if not impossible. Do you remember the last time you had the flu? Rough, wasn't it? You probably found it quite difficult to motivate yourself, and your ability to make decisions that were right for you was undoubtedly impaired. Now imagine how hard it might be to weigh the pros and cons, or *Define Your Wishes* while suffering from a major injury or illness, especially if you are doped-up with a pain-relieving drug such as morphine, or hooked up to life support. I know it's not a pretty picture, but we have to deal with this stuff at some time or another.

If you had an accident, the onus would fall on your family, and they'd be required to make all the decisions for you, facing countless questions from professionals about your health, treatment and care, whilst trying to cope with the impact of this trauma. Would you want to be lying there, unable to speak your mind while other people make decisions on your behalf (especially when *you* could have made them in advance) or do you want to take responsibility and *Define Your Wishes* for your departure? It's your choice. There is much to consider and many questions to be answered. What location is preferable to you: home, hospice or hospital? What treatments are acceptable: drugs, nutrition, hydration or nothing? What to do about family, especially the younger ones?

Do you want them to be engaged or excluded, and who will look after them? Taking responsibility by preparing in advance is actually much easier than it might seem. You can *Define Your Wishes* for the three phases of the end-of-life: *Preparation*, *Departure* and the *Aftermath*.

Be True to You

Preparation — Only you can do this. Preparing for the "what if" is your responsibility. Begin by contemplating what your preferences might be if you were suddenly taken ill or involved in an accident. I've listed a few issues that typically crop up when the time arrives, although there are many other things you may wish to consider:

❊ What have you seen happen to others that you would rather avoid? What have you heard that really got you scared?

❊ Is there a story that wasn't so bad after all, someone whose experience you'd like to emulate?

❋ Will you write an Advance Health Directive or a Living Will, giving someone else the power to make decisions on your behalf should you be incapable of doing so?

❋ At what point would you want nature to take its course?

❋ Will you want a representative from your religion or a spiritual counselor to attend to you?

❋ Do you know the parameters of your health care provider for the provision of long-term or palliative care?

❋ If you were in treatment for any length of time, who would take care of your family or pets?

Departure — Obviously you don't know when this will be but that doesn't mean you can't imagine yourself having a "good" and graceful end. There are certainly plenty of factors that you can determine well in advance. Your first priority will be to ensure that any spiritual, emotional or physical suffering is reduced. No doubt you'll want your dignity and privacy maintained and you will want to be as comfortable and remain as calm as possible.

Picture yourself in a peaceful place, perhaps a hospice or your own home, where comfort, safety and the provision of excellent care for you and your loved ones is the priority. Somewhere that allows you to be surrounded by friends and family, openly sharing your thoughts and concerns, supported by the loving care of great nurses who appreciate your suffering both emotionally and spiritually, as well as physically. You might be quite surprised at the variety of options available once you do a little exploring. You could even go and check out the facilities at your local hospital, hospice, or residential home. Of course, they won't all be to your liking, but that's why it's important to discover what options are available to you now, while you have the time and energy so you can choose the one that's right for you.

Bear in mind that what you think is right for you today may well change, along with the circumstances of tomorrow. Understandably, your preference may not always be available or accessible at the time—if you have an accident you will probably be admitted to the nearest hospital or care facility (but that doesn't necessarily mean you have to stay there). Whatever choices you make, remember to make a family member aware of your preferences or record these in your Living Will or Advance Health Directive. There's really no need to end up in an unwelcoming place, alone and scared.

So you'll want to know if your hosts will help you turn your departure into a positive and comfortable experience, using candles, alternative therapies, music, massage, prayer, rituals, even singing, dancing, hugging and painting—whatever your heart desires. Most people prefer to have family or friends, a therapist, healer, priest or minister at their side, but if you want to, you could have a "special companion," a service offered by some hospitals, hospices and charities. Alternatively, you could talk to The Sacred Dying Foundation or No One Dies Alone who both offer wonderful services for those facing the end-of-life as a lot of personal and emotional issues surface and you will want someone on hand who knows how to help you cope with this. Family, friends and even medical professionals are often ill-informed or uneducated about these aspects of the dying process. "Letting go of the burdens of anger, fear, sorrow, and guilt is an important preparation for death. Time after time I see people holding onto things done and things left undone. I see fear and guilt overwhelm the dying person to the point where he or she cannot let go and die a peaceful death. Most of the guilt has to do with relationships with loved ones. Most of the fear has to do with God," observes Megory Anderson in her excellent book, *Sacred Dying: Creating Rituals for Embracing the End-of-life*.

When the time for departure arrives, the structure of life and normal sense of time will be altered for everyone. Time either shrinks drastically—as an invisible clock quietly informs everyone of the rapidly diminishing minutes—or, it stretches into long and often painful periods as the waiting game begins. Waiting for test results, updates, news, research, doctors, treatments, pills and medications, and maybe waiting for that moment when death finally arrives. Unconsciously, as the final countdown plays out, the question "How much time is left?" persistently beats in hearts and minds. Mom made this very clear in a note she wrote to me:

Gemini,

You know, I had hoped that I'd be the last person to prevent your life from continuing as normally as possible under the current circumstance, but I have to confess that when I heard you say last night that you might apply for a summer job in France, my heart sank. At five o'clock this morning I woke up and cried just thinking about it. I need you near me Gemini. Time is too precious—for all of us—and hopefully there will be other summers in which you can take on the whole world! Even if I was dead, Jacob would need to feel that you weren't very far away.

All my love, as always.

Mom.

Such uncertainty forces everyone into a new reality, altering perspectives, influencing needs, and bending priorities. Fears, beliefs, values, and behaviors change and new concerns emerge. The challenge is how you balance everyone's desires. Because of Mom's request, I remained a Francophile from afar that summer! Thankfully, I chose to stay and care for her—it was only a few months later that she died, and the time during those last months was indeed precious. Her colleagues, friends and family all wanted her time and attention, yet it was rapidly consumed by doctors and nurses, who stole valuable minutes to perform tests, check blood pressure, administer chemotherapy or proffer another miracle pill.

As you might imagine, with so many demands, finding and reserving the time to spend with your immediate family can be quite challenging. Dedicating special time so you can give attention to your loved ones must be a priority, but remember that it's important to always be true to you. When you've found ways to ensure your own needs are met, you will then have the strength, energy and ability to focus on others who walk this path alongside you. Having done all you can to prepare for the inevitable, like the pioneering leader, you are more likely to find a sense of inner peace together with the ability to help your loved ones prepare for the *Aftermath*.

Honor Everyone's Needs Too

Aftermath — In this book, I've already covered a lot of the issues that your loved ones will face after your departure. However,
there are a few areas that I'd like to expand on; communication
is one of them. Your departure is going to be a very emotional
experience for everyone. For most people (even those who seem
to have no problem sharing their feelings), this will ignite fears or
deeply embedded family issues that frequently stop people from
communicating. That's why it's so important to have a mentor or
professional grief counselor who can assist your family. Someone
who knows how to encourage the free expression of emotions and
help them deal with any issues, like forgiveness, anger, and guilt,
that may arise in the aftermath. Be aware that grief support is not
guaranteed in most hospitals, although the majority of hospices
do now offer anticipatory and post-grief support to clients and
their families.

When death arrives, the baton is often passed to your surviving
loved ones, along with the responsibility of what to do with *you*.
But decisions about a funeral are the last thing your survivors need
when trying to come to terms with their loss. You can, of course,
prepare for this in advance and you will learn more about this in
the following chapter. But first I'd like to tell you a little more of
my own story, as I hope this will reveal to you some of the issues
that might challenge your loved ones during the *Aftermath*.

Mom had been in the hospice for a week or so and even though she was receiving excellent care, she decided that she wanted to come home. She wasn't doing well and had been slipping in and out of consciousness all day. Francis and I carried her upstairs to bed where I said, "Sweet dreams, my darling" and wished her goodnight as I pulled the sheets up to her chin, realizing how the roles had reversed— it was as if she were the child and I the parent. After all that terrible pain, the fight and the struggle, she passed peacefully in her sleep that night. The following morning, we sat tentatively on the edge of her bed slowly taking in the scene, her face tilted on her shoulder complete with a gentle and peaceful smile, her skin, no longer pink and radiant, but dull and waxy like the models in Madame Tussaud's, empty of life. She looked so serene. I'd imagined that a dead body would be scary, so I was surprised at how natural it seemed. It was so obvious that *she* was no longer there. Somehow, this made it so much easier to bear.

A few days later, this peaceful parting was marred by an upsetting encounter. We were making our final visit to see her in the Chapel of Rest and we were shown into a small room that was illuminated with candles. Mom had chosen to be embalmed, so she was propped up in a white satin-lined coffin that was beautifully decorated with fragrant pink roses and sprigs of rosemary around the rim. She was wearing the dress I had chosen and her hands were clasped together as if in prayer, her head was resting softly on a pillow. She looked so vibrant, so alive, better than at any time during the last six months of her life. Made-up with cosmetics, her face glowed. She looked beautiful. I was stunned. For a moment, I imagined how she might flash those soulful green eyes and a cheeky grin, then leap up and shout "Surprise!" But, of course, she didn't.

Surely this wasn't the same woman I'd seen lying in her bed just a few days before, this was an imposter masquerading as my Mom; she looked so terribly un-dead! I wanted to reach down and hug her, to hold her, to love her. Instead, I waited until Francis and Jacob had left, then I leaned down over the coffin to give her a final kiss goodbye. It was a big mistake! She may have looked full of life, but her familiar skin, normally so warm, was freezing cold, like stone. I was shocked and repulsed by this deception. The body I had seen the morning she departed looked real and re-laxed and I was comfortable with her death, whereas this version of her body, manipulated into a healthy and vital-looking woman reminded me of how she'd once been. It gave false hope. It was really hard to stomach.

Of course, not everyone has this experience. If there has been a violent accident such artistic license is greatly appreciated and an element of denial is both extremely desirable and perfectly un-derstandable. However, we seem to have bought into the belief that by disguising death we can make it disappear. By creating such illusions, we are playing a dangerous game, because when the truth emerges, we feel cheated, stupid and let down. So please give some thought as to how you'd like to be remembered and consider that the way you *Define Your Wishes* will impact the lasting memories for your survivors. But don't ignore the wisdom of Jill Brooke, who in her excellent book, *Don't Let Death Ruin Your Life*, writes: "If you ask what the dying are most fearful of, the nurses, the doctors, hospice workers and therapists will tell you the same thing. Most people learn to accept the inevitable. They are not scared of dying. They are most fearful of being forgotten."

10

Life Celebration

I can't think of a more wonderful thanksgiving for the life
I've had than that everyone should be jolly at
my funeral — Admiral Louis Mountbatten

It's time to get personal. Everyone's doing it. Personal shoppers,
personal trainers, personal development, personal computers and
personal stylists—the list goes on. These days, almost every service or consumable is prefixed with the word that screams "individuality." We've evolved into a society that demands choice
and lots of it. Not only in our financial services, computers and
our department stores, but increasingly people are requesting a
more personal service to celebrate the end of their life. Take the
family who recently asked the owner of a busy company offering
bespoke funerals for a memorial service on the eighteenth green
of their father's favorite golf course—because that's where he
spent every Sunday. Then there was the group who wanted to ride
Harley-Davidsons down the street scattering the ashes of their beloved friend in their wake.

Interestingly, funeral homes are evolving to meet these changing tastes and will now do almost everything that wedding and party planners do. Bob Biggins, President of the National Funeral Directors Association, and owner of one such company, recently arranged a highly personalized service for Harry Ewell, a man who'd been selling ice cream for most of his life. Harry's ice cream van led the funeral procession and then after the service it was used to serve popsicles to the congregation. "If you call that over-the-top, then I guess I'm guilty," said Mr. Biggins in an interview with the *New York Times,* "but our business reflects society as a whole. Today's consumer wants things personal, specific to their lifestyle, whether it's highlighting a person's passion for golf or celebrating someone's deep devotion to knitting or needlepoint!"

I Did It My Way!

The funeral will inevitably have a lasting impact on your survivors. That is why it's important that your memorial service actually reflects the real *you* and records the special contribution you have made to this world; the lives you've touched and the relationships you've formed, through blood, or love, wisdom or work. It should convey the lessons you've given and the insights you've shared, for which some will hate you and others will forever be grateful. All of this, every second, every minute of every day, every choice you've made constitutes your life, your special time in this world. This is the day when your achievements can be admired and you can be adored. Most of us have never considered how we wish to be remembered, let alone celebrated, but this is your life and it deserves to be honored.

Many people are looking outside the normal traditions, turning their backs on churches, organ music and prescribed eulogies to find a tribute that reflects their personal preferences. Perhaps this shift has occurred because funerals that follow traditional procedure and protocol sometimes feel insensitive to the needs of the bereaved. It used to be that the clergy conducting the service had a long-standing relationship with the person who had died. Nowadays, a lot of people move away from their childhood homes and families, and many consider themselves "spiritual" rather than religious, so they don't belong to a particular faith. This can mean that funeral ceremonies are delivered by someone who has spent fewer than five minutes learning the brief background history of the person who has died. Not surprisingly, the resulting service can come off as a rather impersonal or anonymous affair. This can be extremely painful for the surviving family members—exacerbating their grief and making them feel that the final farewell was a farce. This is a real shame, because it doesn't have to be this way.

In *Funerals and How to Improve Them*, Dr. Tony Walter, author and Professor of Death Studies at the Center for Death and Society, Bath University, writes: "You do not have to have a religious service: you do not have to have hymns; you do not have to have a professional person take you to the service; you do not have to have a religious building, a hearse or an undertaker." It really is up to you. This is your one and only chance to say goodbye, so it should be done in the way that suits you—an attitude that is increasingly being welcomed, even by the traditionalists. Rabbi Kirshner of the Jewish Theological Seminary recently presided over the funeral of a boy whose schoolmates drew colorfully on the coffin as if it were a plaster cast. Rabbi Kirshner said, "Even though Jews are commonly buried in plain wooden coffins, this seemed to be a fitting tribute for such a young congregation." It seems that most religious representatives agree—as long as the personal preference doesn't conflict with religious or local laws, they will make an effort to incorporate your wishes into the funeral service.

Despite this trend, some still make no attempt to personalize or prepare their funeral arrangements—leaving the decisions to their surviving loved ones. However, as with many other end-of-life decisions, this passes a huge burden onto family and friends, especially partners or older children, as they are usually the ones who are left facing the "funeral dilemma," which can be extremely overwhelming for them, especially as they will probably be suffering from the shock of their loss. By taking control and customizing your plans for a funeral or *Life Celebration* ahead of time, you can create a service that meets your personal desires while also reducing the emotional burden that will otherwise befall your surviving family.

You might consider this exercise rather unappealing but I can assure you that my clients have a lot of fun planning their farewell parties. Tony Cornellier was one of them, a wonderful man who had tragically been diagnosed with cancer of the esophagus. Knowing that he had months, possibly weeks to live, he had been planning his *Life Celebration* and preparing for his departure: making a video of his *Life Story*, and creating his *Future Surprises*: writing cards, creating paintings and recording messages for his two grandsons. He left an impressive legacy but it was the preparations for his *Life Celebration* that really surprised me.

Tony had hand-painted a hat-box, something for his ashes to be kept in. The exterior depicted a beautiful landscape of a willow tree growing on the side of a riverbank with a single bird flying high in the sky. Every day since his retirement from his job as a French teacher, Tony had taken a walk along that same riverbank where he would sit under the willow tree and meditate, reflecting on his life. When I asked him about the bird, he told me, "The bird would come and sit in the tree every spring, then one day it flew away and never came back."

When I talked with Tony about his plans for his *Life Celebration*, his life and what he had done to prepare, he was not sad, instead a little twinkle came into his eye. I asked him, "Tony, have you had fun preparing for this?" To which he replied with a great big grin, "You have no idea!" Tony's vision was something he'd carried throughout his life, so when it came to this event it seemed only natural that he should write the following note to his family and friends, which was included in the Order of Service at his memorial ceremony:

Dear Family and Friends,

All of you enriched my life and my understanding of life. Your support, prayers, calls, letters, cards, hugs and kisses and especially the tenderness you showed me, made me feel honored, respected, accepted and loved. As Antoine de Saint Exupéry wrote in The Little Prince. . . "L'essentiel est invisible pour les yeux" (What is essential is invisible to the eye) — Among my essentials are honor, respect, acceptance and love.

Thankfully yours,

Tony Cornellier
(November 1939 – September 2007)

The Beauty of Balloons

Like Tony, and many others, my Mom didn't want a typical funeral with everyone dressed in black or hymns that the congregation found virtually impossible to sing. She wanted the event to represent the life she'd lived and to share with us the fun she'd had. Unbeknownst to us, she had secretly planned her *Life Celebration* some time in the months before her death. The handwritten notes were left in an envelope with the instruction, "To be opened when I'm gone." They detailed everything: the music, a charity for donations, her preference for flowers, a list of invitees, the inscription for her epitaph, readings, poems and even an unusual request for helium balloons. We were surprised and somewhat relieved. We began implementing the plans at once, sending invitations according to her list of invitees, searching for the songs she had requested, visiting the funeral directors to choose a headstone and meeting with the priest to get approval for the balloons. There was so much to do!

It was, however, a welcome distraction from the overwhelming feelings of grief that were beginning to surface. To my surprise, the day of the service came around very fast. It was a bright, crisp day in early November, a week or so after Mom had passed. The gray skies of the past days had miraculously cleared and the sun streamed through the curtains—perfect weather, just as Mom would have wanted. I lay in bed for a while reflecting on the peculiarity of the day that was to follow. I was full of mixed emotions: excitement, sadness, apprehension and astonishment. It still hadn't sunk in that this was Mom's final farewell.

We entered a church packed with hundreds of people. Because everyone was dressed in bright colors rather than black, it really did look like a celebration. The helium balloons that Mom had requested were bobbing above the ribbons that attached them to the end of each pew; light blue ones to represent the sky, green for the earth, and a darker shade of blue for the sea. This personal touch was a vibrant addition to the rather sombre church interior. Respighi's, *The Birds* filled the air as we proceeded down the aisle. There was something surreal about the scene before me —Mom's coffin was set in the vestibule, covered with a beautiful arrangement of lilies which was illuminated by a glorious sunbeam streaming through a stained glass window—it had me fighting back the tears.

Mom had not been one for organized religion, so instead of the vicar reading the eulogy, she had requested three people give speeches to celebrate the many elements and achievements of her life. Ted Coleman, her first boss who trained her to become a journalist at the Skegness Standard, her colleague Dr. Pamela Ashurst and finally, her partner and best friend, Francis. They each shared stories and paid homage to the various identities of Mom: Andrea Adams; author and expert, Annie; aunt and sister, Totty; friend of many. These revealing insights took us on quite a journey. Momentarily we were dropped into the tragedy of our loss then we were filled with laughter as a joyous memory pulled our contorted brows into beaming grins.

Mom chose three popular songs and two hymns; music that she felt had an appropriate message. "The Lord of the Dance" and "The King of Love My Shepherd Is" were cheerily sung by the congregation. But it was the words of her chosen songs, "Prepare the Way," from the musical *Godspell*, "By the Waters of Babylon" by Don Maclean, and "One More Angel in Heaven" from the musical *Joseph and the Amazing Technicolour Dreamcoat*, that really touched a nerve:

There's one less place at our table,
there's one more tear in my eye. . . .

During the reception, everyone commented on how wonderful the service had been. I overheard someone say, "I've never attended such an enjoyable funeral before!" Mom would have been proud. It seems that there had been nothing to worry about. The day proved better than any of us could have expected. Each element truly reflected the person we all loved and respected. The speeches gave depth and insight into her true essence, the flowers added color, the epitaph captured her deeply caring nature, and the balloons—well they were a touch of magic. More than one person noted that they were an unusual but delightful addition. However, it wasn't until later that we discovered the real beauty that lay in those balloons.

Mom had requested that following the service, there should be a small burial attended only by family and a couple of very close friends. As we formed a procession to leave the church, someone suggested we take the balloons with us. It seemed like a good idea, so we untied them from the pews, and took one each before trailing off behind the pallbearers like a crowd of children at a birthday party; walking, skipping and laughing to the burial ground. Not surprisingly, we received some strange looks along the way. That is just what she had wanted — for us to celebrate in her name. We felt her presence very strongly, giggling and skipping along with us every step of the way, but as we came to a stop, the mood changed and a sense of heaviness settled in as we huddled around the empty grave. The priest sensitively read the committal: "We commit this body to the ground, earth to earth, ashes to ashes, dust to dust," and at Mom's request scattered rose petals over the coffin as it was lowered into the ground. The finality of it all suddenly set in.

What a relief when Jacob released his dark blue balloon and it slowly began to rise. Following his lead, the rest of us let the ribbon slip through our fingers as we released our balloons skywards. Drifting in the breeze, one caught on a gust of wind and lodged itself in a tree while the other twenty or so balloons made their ascent heavenwards. Our eyes lifted up from the dark clay, into the backdrop of a vast and clean bright blue sky only to find it full of Mom and her dancing spirit traveling on. We were mesmerized. Our gaze fixed on those tiny little dots, until they turned into pinpricks and then slowly began to fade away. It was sublime. The vicar, despite being witness to thousands of burials, was lost for words. Later when capable of summing up the experience he just said "Oh my . . . those beautiful balloons."

Balancing Beliefs, Tradition and Religion

On that November day, we successfully delivered Mom's *Life Celebration* according to her vision. She would have been so pleased to see us all enjoying her special day—a wonderful and momentous occasion. We were certainly grateful that she had taken the time to plan ahead, and I'm sure that had she not done so, the event would have been entirely different. Her advance planning really took the pressure off, even though we still had to do a lot of organizing in order to fulfill her wishes. The funeral directors weren't really set up to source CD's, helium balloons or rose petals, and the church wasn't equipped with an audio-visual system, so we had to source these things. Even though Mom had made personal requests for her *Life Celebration*, she still incorporated some of the more common funeral rituals and traditions. The priest did give a reading; he said prayers and gave the committal. There were flowers and cards, an Order of Service and a reception in the village hall. The priest and the funeral directors were of great help in these matters and were particularly supportive and sensitive when it came to choosing the casket and headstone, which we had engraved with the epitaph Mom requested:

Andrea Adams

(1946 – 1995)

Who Loves Her Children

Who Fought for Many

Against Injustice

She had managed to successfully balance her personal desires with the traditions of the church. This is something we should all aim to achieve, while also reflecting the traditions of our family, religion or community. Individualization is certainly important, but it's essential to respect your family's needs and give some thought to how your decisions will impact those left behind. While you might think it amusing to have Queen's hit song, "Another One Bites the Dust" played in the crematorium as your casket disappears behind the curtains, others might not share the joke!

Each religion has clearly-defined rituals for funerals, which are primarily designed to honor the dead while also helping the mourners to release the deceased and their grief. While some may find that these are impersonal or dull, these rituals often bring a sense of sacredness and a comforting aspect to the service. These time-honored traditions should be respected as they serve a powerful purpose. If you are not religious there are still options available to you. Rather than a priest or rabbi presiding over your funeral you could arrange for a celebrant or officiant to oversee the ceremony, someone who can conduct the proceedings in accordance with your "voice" but who doesn't need to include any religious references.

You might also want to give some thought to the many alternative burial options from the more common cremation and scattering of ashes, to the super-deluxe packages, which include embalming and fiberglass caskets in all manner of shapes and sizes. In some parts of the world, it is traditional for the coffin to represent the person's trade. For example, in Ghana one sculptor helps local fishermen to rest peacefully inside crab-shaped caskets! For those seeking a "sleep in the deep" there is an emerging American trend for reef burials. The urn holding the ashes is encased in concrete, with an inscription fixed to the exterior, before being lowered to the seabed. Companies offering the service refer to this as a "living memorial." Unusual yes, but not very practical, as your loved ones will have to scuba-dive down to visit your watery grave! For those seeking an environmentally friendly option, the best solution is a green burial in a biodegradable casket where your body can be reunited with the earth "as nature intended." Green burials are becoming more popular in England, perhaps in light of concerns raised by the European Union about the environmental impact of formaldehyde, a potent carcinogenic, which was the base for embalming fluid until it was banned throughout many parts of Europe in 2008. There are many alternative and environmentally friendly burial options available today. If you want to explore these further, I suggest you take a look at the *Natural Death Company* or visit *www.naturalburialcompany.com* and you will find additional suggestions in the Recommended Websites and Recommended Reading sections at the back of this book.

Music is another area where balancing tradition and your vision can be a little difficult. Mom seemed to get the balance right with a couple of hymns and some modern songs. You may want something different from the traditional music; however, this is something that you must discuss with your religious representative to determine what they permit in their venue. You may, therefore, want to enquire about such things where you regularly attend a service, or talk to someone at the crematorium. Religious institutions and funeral providers are becoming more familiar with requests for contemporary music, as a report by the Co-operative Funeralcare found when researching the Top Ten pop songs, hymns and classical pieces that are used most frequently at British funerals. The findings were publicized in the *Daily Mail* together with comments from Ian Mackie of the Co-op, who noted, "Tradition is still very much evident in favorite hymns while we have a growing number of people who feel that modern themes are entirely appropriate. Many now mix the two." The newspaper published the Top Ten chart of *Tunes to Put the Fun in Funeral*, with "My Way" (Frank Sinatra), "Wind Beneath My Wings" (Bette Midler) and "Angels" (Robbie Williams) reaching the top three slots for popular music. The Co-op has also seen a growing number of requests for live music. One of their employees, who is often called upon to sing at funerals, said, "There is something special and powerful about live music, which a recording just can't capture."

Creating Your Own Vision

Having moved into the age of personalization we all want to say, "I did it my way!" This is great, so long as our final-farewell party remains sensitive to the needs of remaining family members. Our choices need to be respectful to their traditions or religion, and should always be designed to bring comfort to surviving loved ones. So how do you go about creating a vision for your own *Life Celebration*? What is acceptable? How do you ensure it will be realized when you're gone? You can start with an idea—simple or extravagant—it doesn't really matter, as long as you reflect who you really are, while honoring the boundaries of local laws and, if you adhere to one, your religion. The cost of your requests should be a consideration, as making requests for professional singers to perform at your service might rack up the expense, whereas having a friend read your favorite poem probably won't cost anything. One way to avoid financial concerns and ensure that your wishes will be fulfilled is to enter into a pre-need or pre-pay agreement with a specific funeral service company. Commonly this is funded by a funeral trust, annuity, or insurance policy and is typically managed by a trustee or insurance company, until the time comes when the money is required. This is beneficial because it allows you to specify your personal requests for the service and burial, while removing the financial burden that will otherwise fall on your surviving family. If this isn't something you wish to consider, you can simply write down the details of the vision for your *Life Celebration* and leave these instructions with your Will and Testament with a good friend, your lawyer or trusted family member.

Try to include personal insights or stories that will leave your survivors with a positive memory and make suggestions for songs, poems or readings that will offer comfort to the congregation. Various studies have shown that when the funeral is a negative experience, or fails to comfort, then the bereaved may experience unresolved grief or abnormal grief as a direct result. This is particularly important for children who are often kept away from the perceived "horrors" of funerals, based on an assumption that they will be scarred for life if they are exposed to death. However, this is not the case. Children who are proactively involved when someone has died will cope far better than those who are protected from the "truth." Whereas children who are shut out of the reality, told not to ask questions, or lied to, are being taught to suppress their emotions, to block the way they feel, and will ultimately find it difficult to trust the adults who have lied to them once they discover what really happened. Consequently, they are often very angry and hurt, and they may experience delayed grief, which can later manifest in a variety of destructive ways.

It is much healthier to explain the "whats" and "whys" of funerals to any surviving children, or grandchildren, and to do what you can to involve them. Depending on their age, you could ask them to draw a picture for you so that you can take it to heaven. You could invite them to bring a teddy-bear to accompany you on this journey or ask them to carry a balloon or flowers to release or place by your graveside. If you can, talk with them in advance about Life and Death issues—you will be surprised at how open most children are on these subjects. Above all, be honest with them. Explain what the event is about and give them the choice, don't make it for them.

This actually applies to everyone. Sensitivity to the needs of your surviving loved ones is essential. It will help if you can involve them in your personal vision. You can do this by holding a family meeting to discuss your preferences or simply by asking your loved ones for their opinion. By opening these subjects up to debate, you help to dissolve fears surrounding the *D-Word*. So grab a notebook (and maybe a glass of wine) to begin planning your *Life Celebration*—the event that will commemorate your incredible life, guaranteeing that you are not forgotten! You can use the following questions as a guide to help decide what is right for this special day:

> ❋ *The Burial*: How do you want to be laid to rest? Buried? Cremated? Scattered at sea? What would you prefer to be buried in, an environmentally-friendly willow casket, a hand-designed fiberglass coffin, or maybe a hat-box? Where do you want the ceremony to be held? At your church, the crematorium, synagogue or temple? Perhaps in a woodland, or even on your own private property?

> ❋ *Rituals & Religion*: What traditions are essential to you and your family? What rituals will you incorporate that are specific to your religion? What meaningful ad-

ditions would you like to include?

✳ *Music*: What message do you want to convey? Do you want traditional music, or something modern, recorded or a recital? How can you incorporate something that will motivate their mood to help your loved ones heal or leave them with wonderful *Musical Memories*?

✳ *Tributes & Memorials*: Is there a cause to which you would like financial donations paid? Will you accept floral tributes or is your preference for something more permanent, like a tree, a memorial bench, or memorial website?

✳ *Readings & Eulogies*: Who will tell the best stories of your life? Do you want them read in person or would you like to pre-record your own message and have it broadcast on the day?

✳ *Offerings*: Flowers, candles, incense, prayers, pictures, flags, butterflies, doves or balloons—are any of these significant to you, and do you want them used at the service?

11

R.I.P
Rest in the Present

*Yesterday is history, tomorrow is a mystery, and today is a gift.
That is why it's called the present — Joan Rivers*

In this book, I've asked you to open something of a Pandora's box, to project yourself far into the future to a rather unpleasant place, imagining something as final as your own death and the agonizing effect this will have on your family and friends. I'm sure that this hasn't been easy for you. That's why I'd like to thank you for sharing this journey with me, for being open to new ideas and for being brave enough to confront your fears of the *D-Word*. It takes a kind-hearted and compassionate soul to reach beyond themselves and seek ways to reduce the suffering for others. *Your Legacy of Love* is one of the greatest contributions you can make to the lives of your family and friends. You could not leave anything more precious behind. By taking the time to read this book and follow the guidance, you have undoubtedly completed a self-less and loving act. For this, I applaud you.

Blessings in Disguise

It is inevitable that while reading, thinking and preparing to share your *Emotional Assets* in *Your Legacy of Love* that many questions will have arisen, together with unpleasant thoughts, worries and disturbing feelings. I said this journey would be challenging, so don't say I didn't warn you! Even more reason to congratulate you for continuing to read on, even when it got uncomfortable. However, I do have a lingering concern. Maybe the experience of reading this has left you with some residual fears and concerns of the impact your death will have on those you hold dear. It would be terrible if you were left in a state of anxiety about something that might not happen for many, many years. So I want to help you dissolve these fears. If you are to *Realize the Gift in Goodbye* you must first begin to recognize the importance of today, rather than being caught up in the "what if" of tomorrow. That's why it's so important to find a positive focus, so you can really make the most of this present.

None of us really knows how long we have left to live. Even when doctors have given a terminal diagnosis, many people live way beyond these predictions; Mom was given three months, and yet somehow she carried on for a further two and a half years. We all have an opportunity to make the most of the life we have, and at the very least, we can try to find a sense of joy and fulfillment in the time we get to spend here on mother earth. If you are in a constant state of anxiety about what is going to happen twenty or forty years from now, this is something you will struggle to achieve. But this kind of fear can actually be used positively, as a source of motivation; to help you follow your dreams and desires. If you can turn your fear of the *D-Word* into an appreciation of life and the opportunity you have to live, it can encourage you to make amends or improvements to your life, your society and yourself. Archbishop Desmond Tutu, winner of the 1994 Nobel Peace Prize, commented on this deep sense of appreciation that often overwhelms those who have received a terminal diagnosis: "It concentrates the mind wonderfully. It gives a new intensity to life. You discover how many things you have taken for granted — the love of your spouse, the Beethoven symphony, the dew on the rose, the laughter on the face of your grandchild."

Like you, I hope that my life will continue for many years to come. I'm a perfectly healthy woman in my thirties. I don't work in a profession where my life is genuinely at risk and, apart from a love of traveling, I don't have any dangerous hobbies. Yet I have a strong appreciation of life and its fragility. The more I have researched the supposedly macabre subjects of death, dying, grief and bereavement, the more I have encountered a strange lightness of being. It came to my attention that many aspects of life that I once considered normal are in fact far more than that; they are utterly incredible. When you take a moment to really look at what you've got, you cannot help but appreciate the quality of life you have and the incredible opportunity you have to do something special with your life. Unfortunately, many of us get stuck looking in the rear-view mirror at what happened to us yesterday, or we become fixed on the conquests or achievements of tomorrow, which makes it difficult to appreciate the gift of the present. We fail to notice the beauty in what we have today, or we grumble about what we do or don't have, forgetting just how lucky we really are. Many of us suffer from a phenomena of perceived misfortune, but it's nothing that a dose of reality can't cure. Stephen Eardley's poem will give you a gentle reminder of *How Blessed Are You*:

If you woke up this morning with more health than illness, you are more blessed than the million who won't survive the week.

If you have never experienced the danger of battle, the loneliness of imprisonment, the agony of torture, or the pangs of starvation, you are ahead of twenty million people around the world.

If you can read this message, you are more blessed than over two billion people in the world who cannot read at all.

If you have food in your refrigerator, clothes on your back, a roof over your head and a place to sleep, you are richer than 75 percent of this world.

If you have money in the bank, in your wallet, and spare change in a dish someplace, you are among the top 8 percent of the world's wealthy.

You are so blessed in ways you may never even know.

I hope you experienced a feeling of deep gratitude and appreciations when reading this. I suggest you tear this page out and stick it somewhere prominent, like your bathroom wall or the outside of your fridge. Because, if you read this daily it will change your focus, helping to bring perspective to your situation while encouraging you to appreciate what matters most—living your life lovingly. You cannot do this when filled with "poor me" thoughts and worries about what will happen to you or your family. Life is for the living, and your situation, however hard it may seem, will always bring you blessings in disguise.

What Matters to You?

While reading this book you may have found that you experienced a shift in your thinking. Perhaps you found that some of those ideas, the ones that once seemed impossible, now appear to be a lot more achievable. You may have felt a little courage creeping in, or a sense of daring taking hold. Maybe you've started contemplating how to "follow your bliss," or how to express your talents and true self or take risks that you would not otherwise have entertained. Maybe you have begun to speak out when you might otherwise have shied away. Hopefully you've seen the benefit of ditching that umbrella of denial and now relish, or at the very least are warming to the idea of dancing in the rain! You *know* that you can have fun splashing in those puddles if you make the choice to live a life that matters. In case my words have not convinced you, perhaps Michael Josephson's poem will help you realize *What Will Matter*:

Ready or not, some day it will all come to an end.

There will be no more sunrises, no minutes, hours or days. All the things you collected, whether treasured or forgotten will pass to someone else.

Your wealth, fame and temporal power will shrivel to irrelevance. It will not matter what you owned or what you were owed. Your grudges, resentments, frustrations and jealousies will finally disappear. So too, your hopes, ambitions, plans and to-do lists will expire. The wins and losses that once seemed so important will fade away.

It won't matter where you came from or what side of the tracks you lived on at the end. It won't matter whether you were beautiful or brilliant. Even your gender and skin color will be irrelevant.

So what will matter?

How will the value of your days be measured?

What will matter is not what you bought but what you built, not what you got but what you gave. What will matter is not your success but your significance. What will matter is not what you learned but what you taught.

What will matter is every act of integrity, compassion, courage, or sacrifice that enriched, empowered or encouraged others to emulate your example. What will matter is not your competence but your character. What will matter is not how many people you knew, but how many will feel a lasting loss when you are gone.

What will matter is not your memories but the memories that live in those who loved you. What will matter is how long you will be remembered, by whom and for what.

Living a life that matters doesn't happen by accident. It's not a matter of circumstance but of choice.

Choose to live a life that matters.

What really matters are those three little words, "I love you." Because love, like air, water and food, is the fuel for life, the energy that feeds our fire. Love is what human beings seek above all else, essential for our health and happiness, it is something we all constantly require. But the path of love is not always easy.

All too often we find it difficult to express our love and most of us are far too busy acquiring "things"—money, material possessions, people or the love of someone else—to remember that this is what really matters. But love is the only way to a deep and lasting sense of fulfillment, as Marianne Williamson notes in her best-selling book *A Return to Love*: "The experience of love is a choice we make, a mental decision to see love as the only real purpose and value in any situation. Until we make that choice, we keep striving for results that we think would make us happy. But we've gotten things that we thought would make us happy, only to find they didn't. This external searching—looking to anything other than love to complete us and to be the source of our happiness—is the means of idolatry. Money, sex, power, or any other worldly satisfaction offers just temporary relief for minor existential pain."

The message "to love" is not a new one; every spiritual leader who has walked this earth has expressed the imperative need for humans to love one another, yet practicing love seems to be easier said than done. When you think about it, no one actually teaches us how to "do" love. We live in a world where we are taught how to "do" everything else, yet learning how to "be" love is never on the curriculum. This might be one of the reasons why we spend all our time trying to find love from other people. This seeking an external source of love often has tragic consequences, resulting in terrible insecurity, jealousy, fear and hatred. To overcome the pain and emptiness we feel, we try to make ourselves more "love-able"—spending billions on fashion and beauty products, devoting our lives to the acquisition of money or material things in the hope that these achievements and awards will bring us the love of others. Yet we don't really need anyone or anything to feel love—it can be experienced instantly—because we are already fully "love-able." As we share and express our love to others, through loving thoughts, words or actions, the feeling of love flows within and radiates out to those around us. Instead of seeking love from others, we must learn to practice loving others.

Learning to Let Go

The problem is that most of us don't know how to practice or "be" in this loving state. Many of us grew up in an unloving environment, or we had parents, partners, lovers or friends who withheld love from us as punishment. Perhaps this gave us the belief that we were not "love-able" even though we are. Such painful experiences may have encouraged us to close our hearts, to retreat inside to protect ourselves. Not wanting to experience the pain that accompanies the conditions of others' love, we have shut down and gone into a place of fear. This blocks our capacity to feel, give and receive love again. We become stuck in a vicious circle. Because we are living in fear, we resonate at a lower level, attracting people who share a similar state of mind and emotion. Our closed hearts mean that our capacity to share or receive the love we so desperately desire is reduced and so we try to fill ourselves up with material things. We stop smiling at the stranger in the street and give up giving for the sake of it. We forget about doing what really matters and as a result inflict misery on our loved ones and ourselves. Of course, it doesn't have to be this way. *Your Legacy of Love* is one that can be lived every day.

You can start this by making a conscious choice to think and act lovingly, to make continued attempts at opening your heart even when situations of conflict have occurred with family members or friends, colleagues, and even strangers. Practicing love with the people you are closest to must become your priority. If you have been ignoring those quiet intuitive messages that urge you to tell someone how you truly feel, then telling them the truth, confessing your feelings, or showing your forgiveness will not be easy.

You may find that the years of emotional constipation have left you fearing the mess that might occur if you express your deepest feelings or desires. Yet, it is this exact fear that inadvertently stops you from getting the very thing that you most desire: the feeling of being truly loved and connected to others. You can only achieve this when you are choosing to express love, and the more you do this, the more you'll find those fears will evaporate.

Perhaps you've noticed how when you don't share your feelings with others, they fail to share theirs with you. If you stop worrying about receiving love and expend your energies by giving love instead, especially in the places where it is least expected, you will get what you really want. You may find it easier to begin by expressing love to strangers who pass you by in the street, on a train or in their car. You can do this silently by smiling for no reason, appreciating something about them, or just by feeling love for them. I often practice this, especially on someone who is tired, upset, angry, frustrated, jealous, or hurt. Silently, I'll send them a blessing with loving words. I'm always surprised at how often the other person will look up and despite their pain or frustration, smile back even though nothing has been said. If you practice this on a regular basis you will discover the real power of love—for in giving, so you will receive—and soon you'll find that your heart has opened again.

You might be thinking, "What's this tree-hugging, stranger-loving hippie on?" But please bear with me. The reason I want you to choose love now is because of the impact it will have at the end of your life if you don't. One of the most common questions that people ask when they approach their departure is, "Why didn't I love when I had the chance?" When we depart this life, our opportunity to give love on the physical plane goes along with it. If we haven't been forgiving, have refused to talk with family members and ex-spouses or have spent our time in pursuit of the "things" that don't really matter, then the end result is usually one of terrible regret. What remains is a deep sadness over our inability to forgive and a heart-breaking sense of loss as we begin to see that we have robbed ourselves of the chance to freely give and receive love. It is a painful realization. Especially when time has run out, or the distance from loved ones makes it impossible to hold a reconciliation or resolve the conflict. That is why it's so important to cultivate forgiveness, to express yourself fully and seek to see the others' point of view. By choosing to love now, you can guarantee that you will achieve a peaceful state, not only in life, but also in death. It is never too late or too early to start.

Choose Love Now

It took me a long time to reach this realization. Wounded by the loss of my mother's love, I pulled back from the world and closed my heart. It was an unconscious reaction. My love went into hiding. I wasn't living it, so I stopped feeling it. After years of seeking, questioning, trying and failing, I finally found that path again. I was fed up with my failed attempts at finding satisfaction in material things. I wasn't having much luck finding love and I certainly wasn't sourcing it from within. So, on the ten-year anniversary of Mom's death I decided, enough was enough. I wrote her a letter. Knowing that she would never read it, this was more of a symbolic exercise, to free me from the bounds of grief, and release my misery. I attached the handwritten letter to a helium balloon and sent it skywards from her graveside. It read something like this:

Dear Mom,

The grief I've experienced over your death has been devastating. I've felt so alone since you've left. Adjusting to this loss has been

212

the hardest thing I've ever had to do. It's been ten years since you left. Ten whole long years—such a long time—yet I can still picture your smiling face, as though I saw you yesterday. During this time, I've struggled a lot. But now I'm done. It's time to live again. I want to be free from the sadness. I'd like to be in peace. From now on I shall remember all of the wonderful things we did together. How we shared such joy, such love and laughter. It's time I shared these great things with others. And lived my life fully, just as you lived yours. I know you didn't want to go. It must have been so hard. But now you are watching over me. Please stay by my side, and keep me safe. Until we meet again.

With all my love, Gemini-Jo x

I wanted to move from the *Gaping Void* of grief into a comforting place of love. I knew that focusing on all the negative aspects of my life would only bring more misery. I needed to create space for the joy to flow through and the only way to do that was by letting go. I knew that if for some reason my life was cut short, I would experience a deep regret as I would not have shared my truth, or lived fully in love, something that seemed a terrifying prospect to me. I didn't want to be standing at those Great Pearly Gates wishing I could go back and change things. So, ever since then I have made it a "must" to live in love. Of course, it's not always easy; experiences, people, friends and family often challenge me. Yet, whenever I am struggling, something always arrives to remind me of why I chose this path, like this story, which was sent to me by my dear friend Tony Carino:

"Last weekend, my family and I had just left a wedding ceremony in a little town on the Oregon coast. It was a beautiful day and we were enjoying the love of family and friends. The sun was shining as we drove past picturesque farms and dairies, winding our way along a two-lane country road. In the distance we saw brake lights. Nearing the bend, a small car came into view, its front end completely mangled. A big camper van, which must have been the cause, was at a standstill. Sirens wailed in the distance, signaling that the crash had just occurred. No firemen, police or paramedics were yet on the scene. People ahead had stopped and were directing traffic, while others stood around looking dazed.

The damaged car had spun around so that the front end was facing us, the driver's side parallel to our view. Someone waved at us to pass on. Jami, my wife, said that she couldn't look, but my daughter and I did. The girl had blonde hair and looked to be in her mid to late twenties. The steering wheel was right up under her chin, her head and neck wrenched into a jagged unnatural position. The air bag was visible, but her soul was gone. She resembled those mannequins in shop windows, a spookily lifelike figure absent of energy. It must have happened so fast. She probably didn't know what hit her. One moment she is driving down a pretty country road on a beautiful summer's day, and the next, she was no longer of this world."

I read this whenever I am wondering why it is that I must forgive the person who has just done something that seems so utterly unacceptable. This story always reminds me of the simple truth, that life is temporary. We never really know how, or when, we are going to go. That is why it is so important to choose love, not only so you can create *Your Legacy of Love*, but so you can live a life that you can be proud of; a life that will be well remembered. Don't feel that you must follow every suggestion I've made in this book. Implementing just one of these ideas will make a real difference to your surviving family. If nothing else, just write a letter; the words you scribe will be treasured forever. Remember that *Your Legacy of Love* can start today, and that you can begin by forgiving someone, maybe even yourself. Hug someone. Pick up the phone, tell them you're sorry, let them know that no matter what's happened, it's in the past, and today you're choosing a new path: "Yesterday is history, tomorrow is a mystery, and today is a gift." Appreciate it. Enjoy it. Above all, love it. Then you will be free of regret and one day you'll be able to rest peacefully in your heavenly home.

Epilogue

Today is the 7th November 2008, which means that it's exactly thirteen years since Mom died—a number that's unlucky for some—but not for me. Thirteen long, confusing and often impossibly painful years later, I now realize that this experience has taught me a lot. I know that "lucky" might seem a strange term to apply to such a tragedy, but lucky it is, in a hopeful, excited, anticipatory kind of way. When you have experienced this kind of loss, you learn to expect the worst, hope for the best and just keep smiling. You also learn to seek the good in your situations, no matter how bad they seem. Or as my dear old Dad would say, when quoting Newton's third law of motion (which he does often) "For every action there is an equal and opposite reaction,"—which brings me to the main reason behind why I now feel so lucky.

You may have been left wondering about my Dad during the events described within this book, which is no surprise considering that when I sent a draft copy of the manuscript to a well-known family therapist, she emailed me with the query: "What about your Dad? You don't mention him much. Even if he was just a source of sperm, you should give us some detail about him!" As you may remember, I mentioned his absence and explained that, due to my parents' divorce and my father getting re-married and having two wonderful children, he hadn't been able to play much of a role in the day-to-day events of our lives. I left out further details because I wanted to share my story chronologically. Despite his predicament, Dad did what he could to help, but it was very difficult, both for him and for us. We had become more than a little estranged during the years following the divorce even though we visited him every other weekend for much of our teenage years. However, trying to cram a relationship—especially a parent-child one—into eight days a month, with the additional demands of work, studies, individual needs, jealousies and everything else that life dumps on your plate, was more than a little difficult. It meant that relations between us were strained, to say the very least. So when the worst happened it was extremely hard for Dad to step in and suddenly support us, especially as his fourth child was about to be born.

I remember how strange it was on the day of Mom's *Life Celebration*. I was sitting between my boyfriend Jin—a young man who had been so kind and caring during the months preceding her death, someone who had been there for me in every sense of the word—and my father, a man who at the time felt like a relative stranger. At one point during the service, Dad reached over and squeezed my right hand; Jin was holding my left and the contrast between these two people felt so vast. One had been with me during the days and nights of Mom's terrible demise, the other felt like a distant cousin who didn't know me from Eve. Funnily enough, that is precisely why I now feel so lucky. Because, thirteen years later, the man I once struggled to call Dad is no longer a mystery to me. While it hasn't been easy, we have slowly developed a friendship and an open, loving relationship. This has required a certain degree of forgiveness on my part—for his affair and the fact that he was able to walk away from his children and first wife. Also for his behavior towards us during the dissolution of his marriage to Mom, which sadly, left me hating him. This hatred was of course the very thing that got in the way of me having a healthy and loving relationship with him. If Mom had not died, I don't think there would ever have been a strong enough reason to look inside my heart and remove those barbs. I'm sure that, as a result, I would have continued nurturing this vitriol until my own dying day.

I once rationalized, in a spiritual kind of way, that in another realm before Mom was born, she was shown two images of how her life could be. The first was of her living a long life, well into old age. She witnessed her children, my brother and me, developing into successful high-achievers, meeting everyone's expectations, yet we were selfish and without compassion for others. She was shown how as adults, we would take from the world, but give back very little in return. In contrast, the second image depicted the progression of her children's lives if she chose to give up her life. Mom could hardly watch as she witnessed the suffering of our grief and the terrible wrenching of our loss. Then she saw how we slowly gained a deeper sense of understanding, developed empathy and a desire to help others who were in pain, or less fortunate than ourselves. She watched in awe as we discovered the beauty and force of love, the most important and powerful lesson of all. She saw how eventually her children would rise out of their despair holding a beacon of light to shine the way for others. I imagined how, filled with maternal love, and in her typically unselfish style, she made the impossible choice—to surrender her life, knowing that somehow it would improve the lives of others. It took me a long time to learn some of the lessons of the past thirteen years and then to birth this book, but I know that I couldn't have done any of it if she were still alive. So really this book is a gift from her, as she speaks through me to you, parent to parent, partner to partner, as a wife to her husband, a mother to her children, and lover to beloved. I hope you have heard the message within and understand that love actually is the most important thing of all.

Acknowledgements

Thank you just isn't enough for the time, enthusiasm, encourage-ment, and support I've received from everyone—even complete strangers—towards the creation of this book. Please accept my gratitude for your faith, contribution and kind words. Especially those who candidly shared their personal experiences of loss, I really appreciate the trust you placed in me to communicate your ideas and experiences. I must also express my thanks to the Win-ston Churchill Memorial Trust whose generous grant helped me to widen my research, from England to America, enabling me to meet with some of the world's most influential experts in this field.

A very special thank you must go to my editors—Linda Laucella who was my number one motivator, and without whom this book would never have been finished. Also to Finny Fox-Davies who so generously gave her time and wisdom to help me turn this book into a complete product. I must also thank Sloan de Forest, Audrey Dundee Hannah and Rashi Mehra whose expert skills in proofreading have left this book 99.99% error free.

Aside from the professionals who have worked their magic, this book would not have come about had it not been for the many friends who've provided me with an endless supply of love and understanding along the way. I cannot thank you enough. Specifically, my dear girlfriends: Candice, Vicky, Ayesha, Melanie and Amanda, as well as the entire SWGS posse, your enduring friendship means the world to me, especially Mistress Mo, a dear friend who has shared more adventures with me than most. My sincere thanks also go to Miles Bullock for helping me conceive the idea for this book while adventuring to the island of Patmos, and to Tony Carino for holding my hand and sharing the mystery of this cosmic journey. Also a big thank you to the Thompson family for inviting me into their home, hearts and lives. To Matthew Joynes, for supporting me and knowing me better than I know myself! I am also grateful to David Block (my official Guardian Angel) who helped me dispel all sense of spiritual amnesia. To those who helped me through the difficult times, Jin Obhi, Allyson Rubin, Charlotte and Nathan. And, last, but by no means least, I want to say a very special thanks to Rebecca Turk — my dear friend and sanity sister. Also to Chris Sanchez, whose unwavering support kept me feeling safe, capable and able, your limitless love has been invaluable to me.

A very special thank you must also go to Guy Holmes, for being my knight in shining armor, my soul mate and No 1 fan of this book! And finally my dear family; you have always been there for me, especially my Granny Hambly — thank you for your prayers, but most of all, for showing me the path of unconditional love, and, of course to Mom, thank you for giving up your life so this book could be written to help others.

Recommended Viewing

Films About the D-Word!

City of Angels (1998)

Death Takes a Holiday (1934)

Flatliners (1990)

Ghost (1990)

Meet Joe Black (1998)

Philadelphia (1993)

The Sixth Sense (1999)

The Five People You Meet in Heaven (2004)

Films to Inspire Future Surprises

Billy Elliot (2000)

My Life (1993)

P.S. I Love You (2007)

Pay It Forward (2000)

The Bucket List (2007)

The Final Cut (2004)

The Ultimate Gift (2006)

To Gillian on Her 37th Birthday (1996)

Vanilla Sky (2001)

Films About Grief

A Walk to Remember (2002)

Always (1989)

Bambi (1942)

Corrina, Corrina (1994)

Grace is Gone (2007)

In the Bedroom (2001)

Life As a House (2001)

Ordinary People (1980)

Message in a Bottle (1999)

My Girl (1991)

Permanent Record (1988)

Reign Over Me (2007)

Steel Magnolias (1989)

Stepmom (1998)

Terms of Endearment (1983)

Things We Lost in the Fire (2007)

Truly Madly Deeply (1990)

What Dreams May Come (1998)

You Can Count On Me (2000)

Recommended Reading

Books About Grief and Bereavement

Never the Same, Donna Schuurman
How to Go On When Someone You Love Dies, Therese Rando
Life After Loss, Bob Deits
Telling a Child About Death, Edgar Jackson
When Parents Die: A Guide for Adults, Edward Myers
Teen Grief Relief, Dr. Heidi Horsley and Dr. Gloria Horsley
Don't Let Death Ruin Your Life, Jill Brooke
When Parents Die, Rebecca Abrams
Continuing Bonds, Dennis Klass
A Grief Observed, C. S. Lewis
*The Grief Recovery Handbook: The Action Program for Moving
Beyond Death, Divorce and Other Losses*, John W. James and
Russell Friedman
I Don't Know What to Say, Robert Buckman
The Courage to Grieve, Judy Tatelbaum
Good Grief, Carol Lee
On Grief and Grieving, Elisabeth Kübler-Ross
When Children Grieve, Russell Friedman, John James
and Leslie Landon Matthews, Ph.D.

Books About the D-Word!

The Denial of Death, Ernest Becker

The Tibetan Book of Living and Dying, Sogyal Rinpoche

Final Gifts, Maggie Callanan & Patricia Kelley

What Dying People Want, David Kuhl, M.D

Attending the Dying, Megory Anderson

Sacred Dying, Megory Anderson

On Death and Dying, Elisabeth Kübler-Ross

Death: The Final Stage of Growth, Elisabeth Kübler-Ross

A Time for Listening and Caring, Christina M. Puchalski,

M.D*Who Dies: An Investigation into Conscious Living and Dying*, Stephen Ondrea Levine

The Welcome Visitor, John Humphries

Books About Near Death Experiences

Life After Life, Raymond Moody, JR., M.D

Closer to the Light, Melvin Morse

Coming Back to Life, P.M.H Atwater

Lessons from the Light, Kenneth Ring, Caroline Myss Ph.D

Dying to Live: Science and NDE's, Susan Blackmore

On Life After Death, Elisabeth Kübler-Ross

Children of the Light, Brad and Sherry Steiger

Beyond Death: Visions of the Other Side, Edgar Cayce

Books About Following Your Bliss

The Purpose of Your Life, Carol Adrienne & James Redfield

Find Your Purpose: Change Your Life, Carol Adrienne

Feel the Fear and Do it Anyway, Susan Jeffers, Ph.D

What Color is Your Parachute, Richard Nelson Bolles

The Power of Intention, Dr. Wayne Dyer

Pathways to Bliss, Joseph Campbell

Discover Your God Given Gifts, Don & Katie Fortune

Joy Is My Compass, Alan Cohen

Spiritual Liberation: Fulfilling Your Soul's Potential,
Michael Bernard Beckwith

Books on Good Guidance

The Loss of a Life Partner, Carolyn Walter

Guidance of Young Children, Marian C. Marion

The Single Parent's Handbook, Rachel Morris

Gay Widowers, Michael Schernoff

Lesbian Widows, Vicky Whipple

Creative Interventions for Bereaved Children, Liana Lownstein

Comforting the Bereaved, Warren and David Weirsbe

Dealing with Death, Funerals and Wills, Roger Jones

What to Do When Someone Dies, Nicci French

The Inheritors Handbook: A Definitive Guide for Beneficiaries,
Dan Rottenberg

Books to Inspire Future Surprises

P.S. I Love You, Cecilia Ahern

Billy Elliot, Lee Hall

Things I Want My Daughters to Know, Elizabeth Noble

The Last Lecture, Randy Pausch

An Hour to Live, An Hour to Love, The True Story of the Best Gift Ever Given, Richard and Kristine Carlson

For One More Day, Mitch Albom

Letters to Sam: A Grandfathers Lessons on Love, Loss and the Gifts of Life, Daniel Gottileb

The Ultimate Gift, Kim Stovall

Shadow in Tiger Country, Louise and Tim Arthur

Books to Help with Your Life Story

Your Life As Story, Tristine Rainer

To Our Childrens' Children, Bob Greene

Legacy: A Guide to Writing Personal History, Linda Spence

How to Write Your Life Story, Ralph Fletcher

Scrapbooking Your Family History, Laura Best

Living Legacies: How to Write and Illustrate Your Life Stories, Duane Elgin & Coleen Ledrew

Grandparents Book: Answers to a Grandchild's Questions, Milton Kamen

Books About Music and Motivation

This is Your Brain on Music, Daniel J. Levitin
Emotion and Meaning in Music, Leonard B. Meyer
The Developmental Psychology of Music, David Hargreaves
The Healing Power of Sound, Mitchell L. Gaynor
Healing Sounds, Jonathon Goldman
The Mozart Effect Don Campbell
The World in Six Songs, Daniel J. Levitin
Sacred Sounds, Ted Andrews
*The Mozart Effect: Tapping the Power of Music to Heal
the Body, Don Campbell*
Musicophilia, Oliver Sacks

Books to Help Define Your Wishes

Choices at the End-of-life, Linda Norlander
Final Choices: Making End-of-life Decisions, Lee Noorgard
Compassion in Dying, Barbara Coombs Lee
Get It Together, Melanie Cullen and Sahe Irving
Living Will, Living Well, M. Dianne Godkin
The Best Way to Say Goodbye, Stanley A. Terman
Death and Dignity, Timothy E. Quill
To Die Well, Sidney Wanzer and Jospeh Glenmullen
Dying Well, Ira Byock
What Dying People Want, David Khul

Books About Life Celebrations

The Party of Your Life, Erika Dillman

Remembering Well: Rituals for Celebrating Life, Sarah York

Planning a Celebration of Life: A Simple Guide, Todd Little

The Natural Death Handbook, Josefine Speyer

I Died Laughing, Lisa Carson

Funerals and How to Improve Them, Tony Walter

Grave Matters, Mark Harris

Final Celebrations, A Guide for Personal and Family Funerals, Kathleen Sublette

Books About Living in Love

Loving What Is, Byron Katie

A Return to Love, Marianne Williamson

The Path to Love, Deepak Chopra

Love Without Conditions, Paul Ferrini

The Five Languages of Love, Gary Chapman

Living in the Heart, Paul Ferrini

Love: What Life is All About, Leo F. Buscaglia

The Love Dare, Stephen and Alex Kendrick

The Mastery of Love, Don Miguel Ruiz

Strength to Love, Martin Luther King

Boundless Love, Miranda Holden

Messages from the Masters, Brian Weiss

Recommended Websites

Get to Grips with Grief Websites

Beyond Indigo was listed as 'Best of the Web' by Forbes magazine, not once, but six times, visit: **www.beyondindigo.com**

Compassionate Friends is a non-profit offering support to bereaved parents, visit: **www.compassionatefriends.org**

Dougy Center for Grieving Children and Families is the leading organization for family grief support in the USA, visit: **www.dougy.org**

Griefnet is a supportive online community of people who are dealing with a major loss, visit: **www.griefnet.org**

Living with Loss publishes articles and resources for the bereaved in both an online and print magazine, visit: **www.bereavementmag.com**

Open to Hope help those who have experienced a loss to cope with their pain and find hope for their future, visit: **www.opentohope.com**

The Grief Recovery Institute has a brilliant action program for moving beyond loss, visit: **www.grief.net**

The First 30 Days feature experts who can help people move through loss, visit: **www.thefirst30days.com**

Veterans Affairs offers advice to war pensioners, war widows and their dependents, visit: **www.va.com**

Widow Net offers support for women, visit: **www.widownet.org**

Dealing with the D-Word Websites

Association for Death Education and Counselling has 2,000 members including medical health personnel, educators, clergy, funeral directors and volunteers, visit: **www.adec.org**

Alzheimers Association offers brilliant advice on this disease and how to deal with it, visit: **www.alz.org**

Cancer Hope Network offers help and advice to cancer patients and their families , visit: **www.cancerhopenetwork.org**

Death & Dying gives Buddhist insight on how to approach this subject in a more holistic way, visit: **www.death-and-dying.org**

Growth House offers award-winning resources for coping with life-threatening illness and end-of-life care, visit: **www.growthhouse.org**

Near Death has hundreds of articles an links to information on near death experiences, visit: **www.near-death.com**

Sacred Dying aims to transform the dying experience, offering volunteers to sit vigil at your bedside to help you make a peaceful transition, visit: **www.sacreddying.org**

Senior Journal is a place where you can explore everything about aging, visit: **www.seniorjournal.com**

The Natural Death Center publishes various guides including the Natural Death Handbook, an extensive manual for improving the quality of living and dying, visit: **www.naturaldeath.org.uk**

Future Surprise Websites

Flowers is the place to order a floral gift to send anytime, anywhere in the world, visit: **www.1800flowers.com**

Inkubook is great for photobooks, visit: **www.inkubook.com**

The Comfort Company have a wide range of ideas that can be sent to your loved ones, visit: **www.thecomfortcompany.net**

Memory Bears are a wonderfully comforting gift, especially for young children, visit: **www.cherishedmemorybears.com**

Memorial Stars will help loved ones remember you every time they see the night sky, visit: **www.memorialstars.com**

Personalized Jewelry allows you to leave them a meaningful message that will always be with them, visit: **www.limogesjewelry.com**

Shutterfly is the place for all your photographic gift needs, visit: **www.shutterfly.com**

Talking Products offers a range of gift items that will let you record your own voice message, visit: **www.talkingproducts.com**

Tree In A Box has a range of trees and bushes that can be sent with a personalized message, visit: **www.treeinabox.com**

With Love From has beautiful gifts that can be engraved with a loving message, visit: **www.withlovefrom.com**

Things Remembered has an incredible range of beautiful gifts for loved ones, visit: **www.thingsremembered.com**

Life Story Websites

Celebration-Of is the place to store precious memories using videos, photographs and your story, visit: **www.celebration-of.com**

Life Story Network provides eulogy, biography and documentary services to help you share yourself, visit: **www.lifestorynet.com**

Life Bio has a host of great products to help you share your story with loved ones, visit: **www.lifebio.com**

Missing You is a site where you can create a memorial to yourself, visit: **www.missing-you.com**

Parting Thoughts is a great site where you can share your story online, visit: **www.partingthoughts.com**

Story of My Life is a place where you can create, share and store your story forever, visit: **www.storyofmylife.com**

The Remembering Site allows you to record your life story as it unfolds, visit: **www.therememberingsite.org**

Your Life Your Story has a variety of products to help you preserve your memories, visit: **www.your-life-your-story.com**

The Center for Journal Therapy works with seniors to help them capture their history, visit: **www.journaltherapy.com**

Musical Memories Websites

Amazon has an MP3 music store where you can buy individual songs or albums, visit: **www.amazon.com**

Gift Songs lets you create a song for a special occasion, visit: **www. giftsongs.com**

Jam Studio lets you create and record your own song online, visit: **www. jamstudio.com**

Rhapsody lets you listen to music, select what you like and create a play list or CD to gift, visit: **www.rhapsody.com**

Song Studio is a place where you can order a song for a special occasion, visit: **www.thesongstudio.com**

Tailored Music allows you to create your very own love song as a gift for someone special, visit: **www.tailoredmusic.com**

The iTunes Store is a place where you can access and download millions of MP3's to create your own playlist or compilation CD, visit: **www. apple.com/itunes**

Walmart has millions of songs that can all be downloaded to create your own special CD to gift, visit: **www.walmart.com**

Your Custom Song is a site where you can have a song written just for you, visit: **www.yourcustomsong.com**

Define Your Wishes Websites

Aging with Dignity is a non profit that provide advice and resources to those who want to plan ahead, visit: **www.agingwithdignity.org**

Better Endings has a series of great documents that will help you make the right choices, visit: **www.better-endings.org**

Family Caregiver Alliance offers information, education and services to help you make the right choices, visit: **www.caregiver.org**

Compassion and Choices has the most comprehensive information on end-of-life choices: **www.compassionandchoices.org**

Hospice Care is an international association providing help on end-of-life choices, visit: **www.hospicecare.com**

Living Will Registry can help you create legal documents regarding your end-of-life decisions, visit: **www.uslivingwillregistry.com**

Legacy Writer is the leading estate planning legal document web service in the USA, visit: **www.legacywriter.com**

The Will Bureau is a leading provider of legal services for estate planning, visit: **www.willsandinheritancetax.co.uk**

Parting Wishes is an award-winning site offering everything you need for writing a will or a living will, visit: **www.partingwishes.com**

Your Ethical Will offers help with sharing your values and lessons, visit: **www.yourethicalwill.com**

Life Celebration & Memorial Websites

Funeral Consumers Alliance exists to protect you and make sure you aren't being ripped off, visit: **www.funerals.org**

Funeral Plan has fantastic tools to help you prepare and personalize your special day, visit: **www.funeralplan.com**

Green Funeral Site is an extensive resource for organizing environmentally friendly events, visit: **www.thegreenfuneralsite.com**

Memory Of is the leading online center for healing. Light a virtual candle or create an online memorial, visit: **www.memory-of.com**

Missing You is site where you can create a memorial page and upload photos or videos, visit: **www.missing-you.com**

Much Loved offers online memorial and tribute services to remember loved ones, visit: **www.muchloved.com**

The Butterfly site is a place to locate farms who arrange for butterflies to be released at your celebration, visit: **www.butterflywebsite.com**

The Funeral Site is an extensive resource for organizing funerals and Life Celebrations, visit: **www.thefuneralsite.com**

The Sky Lantern is a wonderful symbol that can be released at a Life Celebration, visit: **www.theskylantern.com**

Living in Love Websites

Celebrate Love has some great articles on forgiveness and relationships, visit: **www.celebratelove.com**

Five Love Languages is something you need to know about yourself, your partner, children, friends and colleagues. It will change your life, visit: **www.fivelovelanguages.com**

Loving What Is features four powerful questions that will change your life, visit: **www.thework.com**

Love and Forgive offers simple practices for love, forgiveness and letting go, visit: **www.loveandforgive.org**

Life and Love TV will inspire you, visit: **www.lifeandlove.tv**

Learning to Forgive will help you find relief from your grievances, visit: **www.learningtoforgive.com**

Make Your Peace by eliminating conflict from your life, visit: **www.makeyourpeace.org.uk**

Real Love is a brilliant website with a host of resources to help you master this mystery, visit: **www.reallove.com**

Self Compassion will help you learn to be more loving a little closer to home, visit: **www.self-compassion.org**

The Center for Non Violent Communication teaches the language of love, visit: **www.cnvc.org**

The Love Dare is a book that will change your life, relationships and your marriage, visit: **www.thelovedarebook.com**

Bibliography

Age Wave, 2005. *The Allianz American Legacies Study*, May 2005.

Alvarez, L., 2005. Farewell with Love and Instructions. *New York Times*, Oct 6, 2005.

Anderson, M., 2003. *Sacred Dying: Creating Rituals for Embracing the End-of-life*. 1st ed. Da Capo Press.

Anonymous, 2005. Pop Replaces Hymns at Funerals. *Daily Mail*, Nov 17, 2005.

Bell, A., 2007. *Christian Huygens*. 1st ed. Bell Press.

Billy Elliott, 2000. Film /Musical. Written by Lee Hall.

Chochinov, H., et al, 2005. Dignity Therapy: A Novel Psychotherapeutic Intervention for Patients Near the End-of-Life. *Journal of Clinical Oncology*, August 20, 2005, Vol 23, No 24.

Critser, G., 2007. The Man Who Will Help You Live for 1000 Years. *The Times*, Sept 7, 2007.

Dignity in Dying, 2005. *A Fear of Dying Alone*, April 2008.

Eardley, S., 2003. *How Blessed Are You*. "Reconnections & New Directions" Conference.

Edwards, B., and Rodgers, N., 1977, Everybody Dance, performed by Chic. Sony.

Friedman, R., and James, J., 1998. *The Grief Recovery Handbook: The Action Program for Moving Beyond Death, Divorce and Other Losses*. 2nd ed. Collins Living.

Gallup, G., 1991. *Public Opinion Poll*. Rowman & Littlefield.

Isaacson, G., 2007. Music: Different Grooves for Different Moods. *Psychology Today*, September 5, 2007.

Jaworski, J., Senge, P., Scharmer, O., 2008. *Presence: Human Purpose and the Field of the Future*. 1st ed. Broadway Books.

Josephson, M., 2003. *What Will Matter*. Josephson Institute.

Kenyon, G., and Randell, W., 1997. *Restorying Our Lives: Personal Growth Through Autobiographical Reflection*. 1st ed. Praeger.

Klass, D., 1996. *Continuing Bonds: New Understandings of Grief*. 1st ed. Taylor & Francis.

Kübler-Ross, E., 1973. *On Death & Dying*. 1st ed. Routledge.

Leland, J., 2006. It's My Funeral and I'll Serve Ice Cream If I Want To. *New York Times*, July 20, 2006.

Moody, R., 1977. *Life After Life, The Investigation of a Phenomenon: Survival of Bodily Death*. 1st ed. Bantam Books.

Morse, M., 1991. *Closer to the Light, Learning From the Near Death Experiences of Children*. 1st ed. Ballantine Books.

My Life, 1983. Film. Written and Directed by Bruce Joel Rubin.

Puchalski, C., 2006. *A Time for Listening and Caring: Spirituality and the Care of Chronically Ill and Dying*. 1st ed. Oxford College Press.

Reiss, M., 2005. Many Happy Returns. *The Guardian*. April 16, 2005.

Rinpoche, S., 1992. *The Tibetan Book of Living and Dying*. 1st ed. Harper San Francisco.

Sanderson, D., 2005. This is How to Bring Up Our Daughter, Dying Wife Wrote. *The Times*, April 26, 2005.

Sleeper, 1973. Film. Written and Directed by Woody Allen.

Tutu, D., 2007. *Believe: The Words and Inspiration of Archbishop Desmond Tutu*. 1st ed. Blue Mountain Arts.

Walter, T., 1992. *Funerals: And How to Improve Them*. 1st ed. Hodder & Stoughton.

Walter N. Afanasieff, 1993. *Hero*, performed by Mariah Carey. Warner/Chapell.

Williamson, M., 1996. *A Return to Love: Reflections on the Principles of "A Course in Miracles"*. 1st ed. Harper.

Index

Index

About the Author

Andrea Adams, a renowned BBC journalist and pioneer against *Bullying in the Workplace*, died from cancer at just forty-eight years old. It was this early loss that gave her daughter, Gemini Adams the deep and painful insights, which inspired this book.

Wishing to re-connect with her mother's love, especially during birthdays and celebrations—previously joyous occasions that had become *Lonely Landmarks*—she yearned for a reminder, something to help her maintain the fading connection; perhaps a letter, a video or memento, anything that captured the affection of which her Mom had once been the source. Convinced that she was not alone, she began interviewing leading experts in the field of grief and bereavement while training with CRUSE—the UK's leading bereavement care organization, where she met hundreds of survivors, and discovered that the desire for continuing bonds—a tangible way to connect with the love of someone we have lost—is, in fact, shared by everyone. It was this realization that inspired *Your Legacy of Love*.

Gemini now hosts workshops on love and loss in her birthplace, the United Kingdom, and America, where she now lives. She coaches families and organizations who need assistance in preparing for loss. She is a member of the National Federation of Spiritual Healers and was awarded the prestigious Winston Churchill Award for her work.

Visit her: www.realizethegift.com

Your Gift to
The Sacred Dying Foundation

The gift of 20 cents is donated to the Sacred Dying Foundation for every copy of this book sold in the United States to help support them in their mission to change the paradigm of how we approach death in our society through educating the public on new models of death and dying.

The Sacred Dying Foundation is dedicated to challenging the way our society experiences death and dying. The Foundation's primary goal is to return the sacred to the act of dying, transforming the dying experience by reintegrating spiritual and religious practices, and to begin changing the way our society experiences death and dying by serving those who are at the end-of-life.

In addressing the multi-religious and multi-cultural practices and beliefs of our society as well as topical ethics issues, the Foundation is an educational organization that provides information, training, resources, counsel, and an international network for those engaged in end-of-life issues.

For more information, visit: www.SacredDying.org

About Live Consciously Publishing

The intention of Live Consciously is to publish the works of creators whose wisdom will be beneficial to the progression and inspiration of humanity:

–   By creating dynamic and entertaining, yet educational and informative, high-quality commercial media products, which can be published, broadcast or distributed across multiple platforms in order to reach an international audience.

–   By ensuring that the content appeals to all walks of life, while targeting the specific and ever increasing audience who are seeking positive transformation and personal growth in the direction of a healthier and happier life.

–   We aim to collaborate with like-minded people who aspire to create a society of highly conscious communities -- where vitality is valued; where acts of kindness and benevolent behavior are rewarded, and everyone is continuously encouraged to share their unique gifts and abilities, in order to achieve self-realization.

–   Our aim is to serve the higher purpose of humanity by helping to meet the urgent need for a society that sees itself and is very easily able to interact as a unified whole by educating and inspiring and encouraging everyone to . . . Live Consciously.

More at: www.LiveConsciouslyNow.com

Our Environtmental Philosophy

At Live Consciously, we are committed to environmental protection and renewal of natural resources. We recognize and embrace
our responsibility to care for and protect the environment. We op-
erate our business in a way that not only minimizes any potential
negative impact we have on our natural surroundings but we also
seek to renew or recycle the resources we use.

Where possible, we are making our titles available in digital form,
as eBooks, audio files and DAISY to reduce the impact on the environment and ensure readers with all abilities, or even disabilities
can consume our products.

We work with suppliers who share this philosophy, such as our
printers, Malloy, who have dual Chain of Custody (CoC) certifica-
tion with the Forest Stewardship Council (FSC) and the Sustainable Forestry Initiative (SFI). Both FSC and SFI ensure that their
practices for harvesting wood are sustainable and do not deplete
the natural resources contained in our forests. Their books are also
made using a combination of soy, water and vegetable-oil based
inks. For more info, visit: www.Malloy.com

Give the Gift to Friends and Family

Visit your local or online bookstore or order copies here!

YES, I want to save 20% on copies of Your Legacy of Love.
For bulk orders (10+) contact us for even bigger discounts.

Telephone Orders: + (1) 310.453.7711
International Orders: orders@liveconsciouslynow.com

**Alternatively, tear our this order form, complete it, and mail
with payment to**: Live Consciously Publishing,

1422, 19th Street, Unit E, Santa Monica, CA, 90404, USA

Name:_____ Title:_____

Address:_____

_____

City:_____ Postcode/Zip:_____

Email:_____

Please send me _____ copies of *Your Legacy of Love* each
priced at: $10.50 (US) plus shipping of $4.00 per book.

Total Due: _____ Card Type:_____

Card Number:_____

Name on Card:_____ Exp. Date: _____